POLSK

***by* Jonathan Lipman**

Polski Sklep, Polish Plumbers,

and other Tales of Poles in the UK

ISBN: 1532901496
ISBN-13: 978-1532901492

For my parents,

Gillian and Norman Lipman

*"People are talking about immigration, emigration and the rest of the f*cking thing. It's all f*cking crap. We're all human beings, we're all mammals, we're all rocks, plants, rivers. F*cking borders are just such a pain in the f*cking arse"*

Shane MacGowan (attributed)

CONTENTS

Foreword

Some of you may have read my first book *Polska Dotty*, an account of nearly two years my Polish wife Marzena and I spent living in Poland, beginning just after our marriage in Krakow in 1997.

In the *Foreword* to that book I promised to write a sequel addressing the experiences of the many Poles who have come to live in the UK since Poland joined the European Union, on 1 May 2004.

Five long years have passed by, and life got in the way, but I determined to keep this promise. Serendipitously, this passage of time has helped focus a picture of Polish life over here.

So, we now know better the places in which Poles have congregated.

We have a better feel for the number who will truly settle here: around 600,000 at the last census (2011), making Poles the largest ethnic group in the UK after the Indian population.

Polish is the UK's third most spoken language after English and Welsh, but there are a similar number of Welsh and Polish speakers, and I suppose only the latter are increasing. Watch out for Polish to become the UK's number two spoken language soon.

Everywhere you look now in the UK there are Polish delis and hairdressers, and an increasing number of restaurants. There are doctors' surgeries, and even a Polish radio station. There are a variety of Polish newspapers and magazines. There are Polish clubs – book clubs, groups of professionals, self-help groups, and others. There are Polish language classes. And there are countless websites dedicated to Polish life on the *Wyspa* (*the Island* – what Poles call the UK) many of which assist Poles in getting on here.

Imagine! Just ten or so years ago, fewer than 100,000 Poles lived in the UK. Many of them were from an older generation who had put down roots here after the Second World War, having fought bravely on the side of the Allies, only to find their own country subjugated by the Soviet menace. For many of them, it would have been dangerous to return home. Since that time, these Poles have integrated into UK society, often into the higher echelons – including as politicians, artists, writers, scientists, and sportspeople. The television presenters Waldemar Januszczak and Mel Giedroyc (one half of *Mel and Sue*), and the footballer Phil Jagielka, are examples of the children of such past Polish immigrants who have themselves made good.

Now, in a rapid movement westward of Eastern Europeans, they have suddenly been joined by half a million and more of their compatriots – mostly the young, looking for better work prospects. Plumbers, builders, handymen, hairdressers, cleaners, doctors, dentists – you name it. If you plonked one of these elder Polish statesmen in the middle of Arrivals at Luton airport on any given day, I suspect their eyes would pop out as a cast of thousands of Poles streamed by.

With the advantage of a similar credo – a parliamentary democracy, Christianity, the shared wartime experience – Poles have settled into UK life remarkably smoothly. They are seen as capable, diligent and polite. *They're* happy enough here, and contributing greatly to the UK's GDP. Meanwhile, noises off continue: the UK has as good a line in xenophobes as most countries. The likes of the *UK Independence Party*

(UKIP) and *Migration Watch* are the current title holders, and are attempting to seize their moment as the free movement of EU migrant workers, that has allowed so many Poles to arrive on our shores, falls increasingly under the spotlight.

I suspect this will dissipate. In the end, however hard the Little Englanders peddle, they will fail to tarnish an image hard won by hard-working immigrants. Soon, most of us will know Poles personally, and I like to think familiarity breeds tolerance, and eventually understanding and affection. The numbers arriving will diminish, and Poles will settle into British society as a niche – larger than before – but accepted.

In the meantime, I have done my best in Part I of this sequel to *Polska Dotty* to describe the remarkable integration of Poles into UK society in various spheres: starting with their arrival in great numbers, moving on to how they have fitted in, their contribution, and their influence on us – all achieved in just over a decade.

Our own quintessential experience of this influx of "new Poles" came when we engaged Polish builders to carry out a major extension project at our home. We just about survived to tell the tale, but hang on to your hats for a roller-coaster of a ride in Part II.

And, for a 360 degree experience, in Part III, I invite the members of Marzena's Polish Book Club to tell us, first-hand, their experiences as immigrants in the UK, including what they, as Poles, think of *us*...

Part I - The Polish Experience

1 - Raining In My Dining-Room

"Sssssssssssssssssssssssssssssss."

"Mmmmmmmm."

"Sssssssssssssssssssssssssssssss."

"Mmmmm. Mmm."

"Sssssssssssssssssssssssssssssss."

"Errr. Er..?"

"Sssssssssssssssssssssssssssssss."

"Wha..? WHA? *WHAT?*"

Awake! To a strange hissing sound.

"Sssssssssssssssssssssssssssssss."

It continued.

Red digits on my bedside LED blazed 3am.

I crept out of bed, and wandered into the narrow landing of our two-up two-down terraced house in Pinner. Marzena and I had bought it 18 months earlier, toward the end of 1999. That was shortly after our return from a couple of years living in Poland, the subject of the first *Polska Dotty*. It was a former worker's cottage, and we used to joke we were the poorest inhabitants of this well-heeled North London suburb.

The noise seemed to be emanating from the second bedroom that gave onto the middle of the landing. That was strange because, while we were having some work done on the house – the cause of the hissing sound? – it was in the bathroom adjacent. I entered the bathroom first, my fuzzy head telling me that whatever was happening – was happening there. I stood still. Nothing – except a continued, now slightly more distant hissing.

I entered the second bedroom. Bleary-eyed, I groped around in the dark for the light switch, and flicked it on. In the illuminated room, the hissing was louder, but there was nothing to *see*.

I left the bedroom, and decided to go downstairs. A noise seemed to be coming from there, too. I stepped gingerly down the steep and narrow stairs: those workers must have been diminutive, or were dainty as ballet-dancers. Down the stairs and into the entrance hall – really just a square metre between the front door and foot of the stairs. Turn right through the door into the living-room. Light on. Nothing. But now a definite dripping noise. I lifted my gaze to the dining-room, situated beyond the living-room through a connecting square arch. It was murky – unlit – but if I was not mistaken...

I stepped forward a few paces, turned on the light and saw... rain in my dining-room.

From the ceiling, steady drips of water were falling onto our beloved Epstein table and chairs. They were part of a set – along with a sideboard and cocktail cabinet – inherited from my Liverpudlian grandparents. For a long time I had thought their provenance was the same Epstein family that spawned Beatles manager Brian. His family had been into furniture, but that turned out to be a red herring: the brand had been founded by Polish Jewish immigrants into East London of the same name. Nevertheless, the pieces constituted a stylish set, a family heirloom... and were now being rained upon!

Quickly, I switched off the main light, which hung from above the table at the epicentre of the flood, and put on sidelights. Electricity and water aren't good bedfellows – that much I knew. I mopped up the large pool of water that had formed on the table top: fortunately its burr-walnut finish was covered by a sheet of glass, and this had protected the table other than for a little ingress around the edges. The ceiling was another matter: it was clearly sodden; the carpet around the table equally so, where water had run off the glass top. I mopped up what I could, and then woke Marzena.

What should we do? It was the middle of the night, but we had little choice: we called Szymon (Simon), in charge of the small team of Poles working on our bathroom. In charge, though we saw little of him, which was a pity, as he was a pleasant young man, together and well-presented. Instead, we saw Wojciech and Lukasz (Lucas). Wojciech was a fine figure of a man – and a fine man: tall, well-built, personable – and able to fix anything. A paragon of *Polak potrafi* (a Pole 'can do'). In contrast, Lukasz had untrustworthy, darting eyes. He was the nephew of the owner of the building firm which employed Szymon. Thus, being family connected - something of a Polish curse in business - he did as little as possible, but was adept at bossing Wojciech about. Wojciech, knowing which side his bread was buttered, never answered back.

Szymon's wife answered the phone, sounding as half-asleep as I imagined she looked.

"Er, hi – sorry to call you now – in the middle of the night – it's Mr Lipman – Jonathan Lipman – I must speak urgently with...Szymon."

"Ok – he's asleep. D'you know what time it is?"

"Yes, yes – I'm sorry – but Szymon is working on our house – and we have water pouring into our dining-room."

"Ok, Ok, hold on. I give you to him."

Szymon answered.

"Ye-es..?"

"Szymon – it's Jonathan Lipman here. Your men were working on our bathroom today, and we now have water pouring into our dining-room."

Well, not quite pouring, but a little exaggeration never did any harm. Anyway, it was plenty wet.

A pause.

"What is above the dining-room?"

"The spare bedroom – which is next to the bathroom."

Another pause.

"You have to turn the main stopcock off."

"Ok – but then what? Will you come and look at this now?"

A bit unreasonable, maybe, but I suppose, subconsciously, I was asking myself if Szymon would attend this crisis at all, or skedaddle. Maybe if I got him here right now, that problem could be avoided.

"It's the middle of the night. I come in the morning. I come early."

I have to admit I was pretty annoyed at Szymon and his merry men. It seemed likely they'd had something to do with the leak. But, in truth – it being the middle of the night – all he could sensibly do was advise me where the main stopcock was, and tell me to turn it off. He duly advised, and I duly did the turning. The dripping slowly dissipated. After further mopping up, Marzena and I retired to bed – but neither of us got much more sleep.

At eight o'clock that morning Szymon came round with a sheepish Wojciech and Lukasz in tow. First they inspected the bathroom: nothing doing. Then they moved to the second bedroom, where the hissing sound had been at its loudest. No sign of anything untoward (well, not there, anyway; the dining-room was under water, of course). Nothing for it. They switched the water back on. The hissing and dripping resumed. The hissing was loudest still in the second bedroom. They ripped up the floorboards. Underneath, they found water escaping from a pipe joint that Wojciech had welded inadequately. This small leak had – over the course of many hours – caused all the damage.

I felt bad for Wojciech. He was a hard and generally capable worker, in contrast to Lukasz – an indolent and mouthy individual. But I knew all about connections from my time spent living in Poland – much of *Polska Dotty* is dedicated to the subject – and Lukasz was living off them.

After some negotiation, Szymon agreed to replace the dining-room ceiling. Down came the old – almost by itself – and up went new plasterboard that then needed plastering and painting. Given that this had been a small job from the start – essentially, installation of a new bathroom suite – it must have taken all profit out of the job, or worse. In the end we paid Szymon a little extra, seeing how hard Wojciech and he, in particular, had worked. I even handed Wojciech my ghettoblaster – an advanced model with a remote – which he'd taken a shine to, and which Marzena had taken equally against (too bulky in our small kitchen). Two birds and one stone.

Whilst what happened with Szymon and his team had been traumatic, it was not all bad. The quality of their work was good (when they weren't leaving holes in pipes). We ended up with a smart new bathroom and, of course, a new dining-room ceiling, freshly painted.

And this pattern would repeat when we hired Polish workers again – in particular plumbers and builders. Generally their methodology would be sound, producing excellent results. But as there could always be an occasional slip – often with disastrous consequences – they needed *managing*. Never would this become more apparent than when, fifteen years later – with an influx of Polish plumbers and builders having long since entered the country following

Poland's accession to the EU – we took our chances with one of them on a major extension to our home. That would be an adventure to make the Pinner dining-room deluge look more like an April shower...

2 - Polish Invasion

Poland joined the EU on 1 May 2004. It was by far the most populous of the ten nations that joined at that time – eight of them from Central and Eastern Europe. Its population of 40 million exceeded that of all the other new members put together.

At that time, just three countries agreed to open their doors fully to workers from the new member states. These were Sweden, Ireland, and... the UK. The remaining EU states imposed transitional controls restricting entry into their countries for up to seven years – the maximum allowed. Famously – or infamously – the UK government of the day predicted an annual influx of just 13,000 from these new entrants.

In reality, of course, huge numbers of Central and Eastern Europeans, and Poles in particular (being the most populous) made their way to Sweden, Ireland and the UK, and the government's prediction of 13,000 per year – publicised, perhaps, for its own political purposes – would go on to cause it more than a little political pain. In fact the figure is unfairly maligned, as the research on which it was based included many caveats.

As the UK had by far the largest economy of the three 'open door' countries, and therefore the most job opportunities, the majority of migrants came here. Perhaps Poles had also been influenced by a creeping Anglicisation in

Poland: English pubs, English signs in shops – and, of course, English being taught in schools. The Polish contingent comprised in particular the youth and rural workers, amongst whom unemployment back home had been especially high. We knew from family members and friends in Poland that it was difficult to find work at this time, and even if you could, wages were extremely low – the equivalent of a few hundred pounds a month. In contrast, unemployment in the UK was low, there were jobs available, and salaries were much higher on average than in Poland.

Many Poles arrived in the UK to take up a variety of jobs. They found employment as cleaners, farm and factory workers, doctors, dentists, and everything in between. You could (and can) hardly find a bar in London without a Pole serving in it (it used to be Aussies). And of course that's not forgetting the builders and the ubiquitous Polish Plumber. Many came on budget airlines, which must have contributed to the influx. Back in the day Marzena and I could afford only a 27-hour coach ride between Poland and the UK – not such an attractive proposition as a two-hour flight.

The Poles settled in urban areas, gravitating to certain towns and cities. The largest were London, Birmingham, Edinburgh, Glasgow, Slough, Southampton and Luton. But they also went to rural areas to work as farmhands, picking fruit and the like.

The Poles were overwhelmingly well-received by British employers. I remember a feature on the BBC's *Newsnight* not long after the floodgates opened. An employer was speaking about Poles he had employed to drive his buses. It was rather ironic. He explained on camera how they spoke good English, and were polite, hard-working and… punctual. *Punctual*, I remember thinking to myself! Isn't that precisely what a bus driver should be? I pictured lazy, indigenous workers swearing at their employer as they arrived late for work. Such a contrast in work ethic was the impression the employer gave.

Young white British men are most derided group in UK

The Independent

The impression the *Poles* gave was one of diligence, enthusiasm, skill and flexibility. Correct, one might say. They often took on low-paid jobs the locals wouldn't, and in many cases worked their way up to managerial positions, be that in the fields or offices. In that hackneyed phrase – but it is true of Poles – they worked hard and played hard. They did not play at work, and simultaneously try to *look* hard-working – a deception, as we shall see later, spotted by a member of the All-Girl Polish Book Club. In late 2015, in an *Independent* article headed "Young white British men are most derided group in UK", the author of the YouGov poll on which the article was based summed things up nicely. "Poles clearly do better", he is quoted as saying. "We think they are more likely to be polite and to help others – and far more likely to work hard."

We'll look later at the vexed question of the net contribution of Poles to the UK economy – vexed largely because a phalanx of Little Englanders will have their say. The latter should watch their words: 585 people were arrested for hate crimes against Poles in the UK in 2013.

That said, one cannot ignore that an influx of Poles has, inevitably, created pressures here. Wages were forced down by the sudden presence of a group of workers prepared to work whatever the conditions – something Poles are renowned for (I remember French port workers getting uppity a few years back at an influx of Polish stevedores, prepared to work for very low wages). We'll take a closer look at that later, too.

The upshot of all this was that the figure of 13,000 – however much misrepresented – turned out to be *wildly* inaccurate. In fact, I heard it said that the movement of people after 1 May 2004 was the greatest migration across Europe since the end of World War Two (though I dare say the current migration *to* Europe from war-torn parts of the world such as Syria outstrips even this). Officially it comprised the people of ten nations moving to three recipient countries. But everyone knows that, for the main part, it comprised Poles moving to the UK.

The statistics are astonishing. In 2004 Poles were the thirteenth largest national group in the UK, at less than 100,000. They were communities that had settled largely in enclaves of big cities, such as Ealing, often linked to Polish pilots and other emigres who had fought bravely on the side of the Allies in the Second World War, only to find the path back home to Poland cut off by the invading Communists. By 2008, the new wave of post-EU membership immigrants made Poles the largest foreign national group in the UK. In that year 44 million pints of Lech and Tyskie Polish beer were being sold annually in the UK! I don't think to Brits...

The 2011 UK census determined 600,000 Poles living here, though many observers, myself included, would have put this figure much higher – maybe nearer 1 million. Indeed, 2015 statistics show there are around 850,000 UK residents who describe their nationality as Polish – the most common non-British nationality. Even at 600,000, this comprises 1% of the UK population. Poles comprise 14% of all foreign citizens in the UK. This gives ample fodder to that veritable arbiter of taste and moderation... the *Mail Online*. On any given week look out for one of their headlines along the lines: "Britain now has as many Poles as [enter Polish city of choice]". Actually, I'll say one thing for the *Mail* - they take more of an interest in the Polish experience in the UK than any other paper, and have on occasion said nice things about the Poles. On occasion.

A large number of Poles are here in UK to stay. That much is undeniable, but the picture is complex. European Commission figures say the average time spent abroad by Polish immigrants is ten years, but in reality of course, many come and go, for shorter or longer periods – and there are trends. That putative figure of 1 million may be a high-watermark, as many Poles decide to return home, encouraged by Poland's burgeoning economy and enticements from the Polish government who wish to reverse this brain drain.

Particularly impressive about the Poles' integration into UK life is their entrepreneurship – something much in evidence during my time living in Poland. *Polska Dotty* is replete with examples, from street vendors who accosted Marzena and me in Zakopane on a broiling summer's day and attempted to sell us thick woollen mountain sweaters, to a gym manager leading Marzena through a changing-room of naked men as the only way, at the time, to show us the facilities on offer (as it were) – not forgetting the computer whizz kid and "lazy" car electrician. The list is endless...

Here, things have been done with equal zeal and aplomb. Poles have set up their own businesses – delicatessens (who in the UK hasn't seen a *Polski Sklep* or Polish Shop?), hairdressers, beauty salons, dressmakers – you name it – and got themselves officially qualified as plumbers, electricians and more. There are Polish GP surgeries, Polish travel agents – even Polish firms of accountants. This is quite apart from the Polish cleaners or handymen advertising in many a shop window. I am pleased to say the Polish entrepreneurial spirit shines on, unhampered by displacement to a foreign country.

Poles really appreciate how relatively straightforward it is to set up and run a business here in UK. When I lived in Poland, Poles complained bitterly about the prohibitive taxes that stymie initiative. One of them, *ZUS* (national insurance) was at a rate of 48%, payable by the employer on each and every employee! Sole traders don't escape the heavy rates, either. Things are supposed to have improved in Poland since then. The World Bank's 2016 *Doing Business* report ranks Poland at 25 overall, up from 28 the year before – and Poland has been one of the highest climbers in this report over the last decade. But Poles in the UK still appear to hold a jaundiced view of bureaucracy back home. And maybe with good reason. The same report ranks Poland 85 in a list of 189 economies for ease of starting up a business.

We personally know Poles who run building businesses, newspapers, and a chain of flower shops, who own furniture businesses, and are qualified plumbers. Our go-to Polish handyman, Konrad, of whom more shall be said later, has just started his own business having previously moonlighted whilst delivering pizzas as a day job. Our cleaner is Polish – the second in a row. There is a whole slew of Polish businesses in the UK, often serving their compatriots, but also the indigenous population. Though I have to say I don't envy the latter. I know Marzena, as a fellow Pole, gets a favourable rate from her hairdresser. And when we purchased a new kitchen from a trade supplier as part of our major building project, the salesman offered Marzena a huge discount, explaining with a wink that his girlfriend was Polish. Maybe as a consequence, he was out of a job a week later, but the company felt honour-bound to maintain his offer.

The increasing integration is fascinating to observe. I have long since frequented Polish hairdressers in the UK because I find their technique second to none, and their prices equally attractive. I just take care not to end up with red hennaed hair – a perennial favourite amongst Polish women. When I first used to have my hair cut at such places, the clientele was pretty much exclusively Polish. I admit I felt the odd man out. But a few carefully chosen Polish words later – including that my wife was Polish (*Mam zone Polke, wiesz!* / I have a Polish wife, you know!) – and I was instantly a member of the club. I'd then be spoken to in Polish at machine gun rate for the next half hour, and would nod sagely every few seconds when the scissors were at a safe distance. I understood practically nothing. But what I observed was a steady increase in the number of English customers. I felt a mixture of jealousy – I was the first "foreigner" here, you know! – and relief for the Polish business owner who may have needed this wider mix of customers to survive. Or maybe not. The majority of customers in Polish hairdressers, delis and the like remain, as far as I can tell, Polish. That's good and natural enough. The question is, can they *all* survive on such clientele? Certainly I witnessed one or two Polish delis in my own town that set up, and were gone within weeks. On the other hand, the sheer number of Poles over here will, I suspect, sustain many a Polish business.

As Poles have become successful, so they have put down roots. They have taken on mortgages and bought houses, bought right hand drive cars, sent their kids to the local schools – and all the other things people do as they live their day-to-day lives. Many have become reluctant to return to Poland. An inertia to moving back develops. After all – as I know some of them reason – what can Poland offer except possible unemployment and a lower standard of living? The decision is cemented as their kids spend longer and longer in

English schools, forgetting what Polish they had when they arrived here. They will grow up and attend English universities, and get jobs here. In the long run, I hazard the EU's claim that on average Polish immigrants spend ten years abroad may have to be revised upwards consequent on the many Poles who will have settled here, and presumably in Sweden and Ireland, too.

All of this has been rather a delight for Marzena and me to behold. When we settled in the UK together in 1999, it was still five years before Poland joined the EU. Polish representation in the UK was scattered between a handful of communities that had established themselves over the years, with Ealing and Balham being a couple of the more renowned. There was and remains a Polish community centre – *POSK* – in Hammersmith, home to, amongst other things, a Polish restaurant, café and bookshop. And a famous upmarket restaurant – *Ognisko* (the Polish Hearth Club) – resides in Exhibition Road. For some reason the *Top Gear* trio ate there a while back (hope they had hot food on the menu). Perhaps of most note, an otherwise unremarkable looking corner newsagent near *POSK* became the repository for endless job ads in Polish, filling the window. It was the place to go if – pre-EU membership – you came to the UK as a Pole looking for work. The Poles called it *Sciana Placzu* (The Wailing Wall).

The point is if you did not live in these areas, you could go a long time without hearing a Polish voice, or seeing a Polish ad or sign in a shop window – let alone a Polish shop. How times have changed! Poles are now settled well outside the boundaries of these traditional enclaves, in all four corners of the UK. Some places, as mentioned, have developed quite large Polish populations, including where there were previously none. The *Polski Sklep* has become ubiquitous, a sign that there are a fair number of Poles – if not a thriving Polish community - nearby.

Whilst I know the vast influx of Poles did not come here for our gratification, I have always felt good for Marzena that it happened. We live in a town with a sizeable Polish contingent, and will always hear Polish voices when we go out. And see *Polskie Sklepy.* And chat with Polish waiters and waitresses in restaurants and bars. Round our way, local authority literature is even translated into Polish, along with Urdu, Punjabi and the like. Marzena has a good chinwag every Friday with our Polish cleaner, belongs to a Polish book club (of which more in Part III), and lives in a house extended by a Polish builder (see Part II) whose connections with Polish infrastructure in the UK – suppliers, labourers, and skilled workers – would be a revelation. Marzena heralds from Krakow in the *Malopolska* ("Little Poland") region of Poland. Our joke was always that our house – filled with Krakowian bibelots and the aroma of Polish cooking – was like a Little Poland. Now, we can apply that to parts of our *town*, and many others in the UK.

And long before all this occurred – before Poles entered the UK en masse and made their stamp on life here – Szymon and his gang were already around carrying out handiwork and minor building projects. Not particularly well, it has to be said; they specialised in causing leaks, and damaging family heirlooms. But they were already here, established, ahead of the crowd. That much, I'll give them.

3 - Home from Home

June 2007, and I took a new job in Slough. It was three years since Poland had joined the EU. Probably as many as 500,000 Poles had entered the UK by then.

My office was on the Bath Road, part of the vast, unglamorous Slough Estates complex where the opening credits for *The Office* were filmed. I remember arriving for interview by car, and noticing amid the endless grey slabs of concrete a yellow canopy on which the words *Polski Fryzjer* (Polish hairdresser) were emblazoned. If I ever get this job, I reflected, that'll be the barber for me. Just down from my office, no doubt cheap and cheerful - and a place to practise my pidgin Polish on poor, unsuspecting Polish immigrants (which I do nearly everywhere).

And so it turned out. Gosia cut my hair for the next five years, at a few quid a visit. During that time I would learn a little about her life, before she got pregnant and went on maternity leave – that she had come to the UK several years earlier, in a first wave of Poles to enter the country after Poland joined the EU; that she had a Polish boyfriend who also worked over here. I also learnt that the salon was run by Magda, who soon opened a second salon in another part of Slough, which I began frequenting, and which turned out to be an eye-opener.

Situated on the second floor of a fresh white painted modern block, at the end of a parade of shops on the

Farnham Road as it heads north out of Slough, the new salon was decked out with typical Polish flair - angular steel and leather chairs, with a slight patterning on the white walls. In the background played – of course – *Polskie Radio Londyn* (PRL, or Polish Radio London), the main UK-based Polish radio station. I had many a happy haircut there, despite having to listen to a mix of Polish and English middle of the road rock.

This was definitely a step up from the first salon, which was on the ground floor of a red brick Bath Road council house - but it was the whole parade of which the new place was part that really caught my attention. When climbing the stairs to the hairdresser I noticed a Polish doctor's surgery on the first floor, and wondered if this might be a sign of a developing Polish quarter in Slough. The parade also boasted two shops calling themselves *Polski Sklep*. However, such signs can be deceptive..! I have carried out an informal study of the famed *Polski Sklep* in the UK, and established there are two types – the real *Polski Sklep*, and the ordinary grocer's shop in which the owner, recognising in the influx of Poles a potential commercial opportunity, has decided to buy in some Polish basics and add the words *"Polski Sklep"* to his shop front. I admire both kinds of shop-owner for their initiative – but the two types of *Polski Sklep*, though they both serve a useful purpose, are not comparable.

The latter *Polski Sklep* – which I shall uncharitably term "fake" – will sell Polish powdered cooking ingredients and soups, Polish chocolate bars and sweets, and oodles of Polish beer (those 44 million pints have to be retailed somewhere). If you're "lucky" there'll be a rather manky looking piece of cake in a refrigerated section.

In contrast, the real McCoy will be akin to a true Polish deli in Poland – maybe even better because, as the only place UK-based Poles can buy Polish food, it needs to stock everything, and at every price point. There will be, essentially, all the variety you might find in a supermarket several times the size in Poland. So "deli", as we know it – a place to buy overpriced stuffed vine leaves, hummus, and "speciality" bread – is more than a tad misleading. The Polish deli will include a meat section stocking – of course – many types of *kielbasa* (Polish sausage). Some are best for cooking in soups, some for frying, some just for eating cold. For example, one of Marzena's and my favourite dishes, *zurek* (sour rye soup), is cooked with *kielbasa* and hard-boiled egg. And yes, you can buy the sour rye in solution in a real Polish deli. You will also be able to purchase every type of ham known to man – smoked, steamed, salted, cured, or a combination. Our favourite is *sopocka*, which is steamed, smoked, and relatively light.

In a real Polish deli, there will be a cake section par excellence. The Poles love their cakes. There will be *sernik* (cheesecake) for which the Poles are famous, *makowiec* (poppy seed cake), *tort orzechowa* (nut cake), *smietanowiec* (trifle) – and many, many more.

The ready availability of so many fresh cakes should not be taken for granted. Before we lived near Slough we were based in Bedford, where at the time there was just one Polish deli. It was the real type, but – shock, horror! - did not stock fresh cakes. Marzena remembers asking the owner if she would ever do so. "Don't worry", the owner told her. "They'll be in soon, when I fly back from a trip to Poland." I pictured the woman stashing bags of cakes into every nook and cranny of the aeroplane's overhead lockers. At the time, Poles were not generally baking cakes and bread locally in the UK. Times, thankfully, have changed...

As well as a huge variety of cakes, a real Polish deli will have a well-stocked sweet counter including Polish chocolate bars – the chocolate and wafer variety are popular – and at least three types of halva: plain, chocolate flavour, and studded with nuts.

And then there are the *paczki* (doughnuts). Polish doughnuts, unlike the stodgy British variety, are light as a feather. They can be filled with custard or rose petal jam, and have glazed orange peel on the outside. At work, when it is my turn to bring in something for our monthly team meetings, I'll invariably present a bag of freshly cooked *paczki*. My offerings have become predictable, but they seem to go down well enough.

Apart from meat and cake counters, the real Polish deli will stock its own fresh bread – often seeded, and dark like German bread. Rye bread is a favourite of Marzena's. They'll have that, too. And pretzels.

And a vast selection of beer.

And the same of vodka.

And everything else.

A *real* Polish deli is a veritable Food Emporium.

Of the two stores claiming the title *Polski Sklep* on the Farnham Road parade, one is a "fake" – but just a door or two down is the real thing, called *Smaczek* (Taste). On an early visit I met its owner, who I mistook for an assistant as he looked all of 19 to me. A charmer, who speaks good English, he explained to me he was about to open another deli in our neck of the woods, which he duly did. At the time of writing I notice he has just relocated his Farnham Road store to a newly-fitted out space that gleams, a few doors down. He's another Polish entrepreneur, and there must be plenty of them in this business alone, because I see Polish delis in most places I visit. After finishing in Slough, I worked for a while in Coventry, and noticed several Polish delis there. They seem to spring up in twos or threes, rather like kosher delis in the larger UK cities that have Jewish communities.

We often frequent "our" *Smaczek*. I've got to know the friendly older lady who serves there, who knows I come for the rose petal variety of *paczki*. A mere smile or frown from her as I enter the shop and I know if they are in stock. She was also kind enough to stick a flier for *Polska Dotty* in her small shop window when I was first promoting the book. She didn't charge for this service, so I feel it's my duty to keep buying *paczki* from her for the foreseeable future. It's a tough ask, but someone's gotta do it.

Smaczek's shop window was not the only place I promoted *Polska Dotty*. Gone are the days when the choice of Polish language publications in the UK was between the traditional *Goniec Polski* (The Polish Messenger) and *Dziennik Polski* (The Polish Daily). Most Polish delis will stock a small selection of books in the Polish language alongside a much larger offering of Polish newspapers and magazines. I could not believe it the first time I ambled into one of the Polish shops on Farnham Road, hoping I might find at least one publication likely to be suitable for reviewing my book.

There, laid out before me, was a cornucopia - free publications, and paid for; colour, and black and white; tabloid, and broadsheet. And I'm not simply talking publications imported from Poland (though there were also a few of those). These were home grown journals, set up in the UK by immigrant Poles. Among them are *Cooltura*, *The Polish Express*, and *Panorama* (all of which gave *Polska Dotty* the thumbs up), as well as *The Polish Observer* (which serialised the book).

Aside from print media, a plethora of Polish websites have been established in the UK, and they contain a wealth of self-help information for Poles living here. Some cover the whole UK, and some are regional, usually aimed at Poles in a big city. Among these websites is *Londynek*, subtitled *the UK*

Polish Community Online, which covers the whole of the UK as well as London. It is a well-presented website featuring news, accommodation, jobs, business, and buy and sell sections, to name but a few. *Polish Forums* is an international chat room whose strap line is *The Ultimate Guide to Poland*. It has a UK section on which anything and everything is discussed. At the time of writing, someone needs help moving art works from Scotland to Nowy Sacz; someone else wishes to transport a rabbit to the UK; a third simply poses the question "Where can I buy Polish beer in the UK?"; and a fourth asks "Why don't the English like the Polish?" The mind boggles...

Poles in the UK have also established clubs – formal and informal – where they can meet face to face. Some are simply local clubs for specific areas of the country, but others are thematic, focused on, for example, sport. So, Polish five-a-side football leagues have grown up in London and Birmingham, building to an extent on Polish sports clubs established by the traditional community that remained after the Second World War (for whom volleyball was always a favourite).

I myself am a member of the Anglo-Polish Association of lawyers. I am also its worst member, as I have never been to a meeting. I *have* watched a video they posted online, which seemed convivial and worthwhile – forging links between Polish and English lawyers at university level and beyond.

Marzena cannot be accused of non-attendance of her All-Girl Polish Book Club. Invited to attend by a fellow member whom she met when retrieving our kids from gym club one day, she now cannot be seen for dust one Saturday night each month. The girls pick a book *po polsku* (in Polish) and discuss it over a cordon bleu dinner of several courses prepared at one of their houses, on a rota system. At least,

that's what they say. Mysteriously, the rest of the hostess' household is always encouraged to go out on the night of the book club, and return home as late as possible. It might just be that they discuss more than the book – their husbands, for example.

I have noticed that Poles in the UK have been slower to set themselves up in some aspects of their lives than in others. This is often for understandable reasons. So, there is only one Polish radio station in UK of which I am aware (the afore-mentioned *Polskie Radio Londyn).* It's a commercial station that I wouldn't say is highbrow, playing mostly rock and pop, and with very little chat. PRL may enjoy a monopoly simply because it cannot be easy to set up a radio station, and the cost and effort to obtain a licence are no doubt prohibitive. In any case, Poles don't seem to worry about the restricted choice. *PRL* plays in every hairdresser, deli and other Polish establishment within reach of London that you will ever walk into.

I have also observed that, increasingly, there are Polish features on established radio stations. So, the BBC may dedicate a half hour on some aspect or other of Polish life over here (later we will look at one such feature in which Poles expressed their views on the UK health service). On local radio, there may be a regular half hour slot on Polish life in the UK. It is encouraging that these programmes are not always fronted by a crusty sounding WASP with a clipped Home Counties accent, but that Poles are often writing and presenting, offering *their* views on things.

Polish restaurants – I mean other than the Polish Hearth Club, which is anyway out of reach of most pockets – have been slow to establish. I suspect a fresh wave of immigrants is more in need of their own delis than their own restaurants. But I have noticed a change latterly. There is a

Polish restaurant above the shopping parade on the Farnham Road, which I have yet to try, others round our way, in Maidenhead, and already quite a few in London. They generally receive good write-ups. Polish cooking does not have the reputation of, for example, French or Italian cuisine, but can be first class. There are staples of the Polish diet, such as *pierogi* (ravioli – but of a superior sort) which seem to be very popular with foreigners. Then there are *golabki* (which translates literally as "little pigeons", but in reality means stuffed cabbage leaves), *placki* (potato pancakes), *schabowy* (breaded pork cutlets)... the variety is huge, and food in different parts of Poland reflects different cultural influences (or as some Poles might say, the tastes of different invaders). There is also a strong crossover between Polish and Jewish food. Many a Polish restaurant will include Jewish dishes on the menu, such as chopped liver (referred to as "Jewish caviar"), or *Karp po zydowsku* (Carp in Jewish style). Both nations, it seems, claim the ownership rights to beetroot soup, *Borscht* in Yiddish, and *Barszcz* in Polish. They are welcome to it - I hate it.

If you think on it, what the Poles have established in the UK in ten short years is incredible. They have made a veritable home from home. Yes, they built on foundations laid by the post-War Polish immigrants – but not to a great extent. Before Poland joined the European Union and large numbers of Poles began arriving here, Marzena – and I on her behalf – often felt isolated from Polish culture in the UK, as the only obvious signs of its existence were institutions such as POSK and the Polish Cultural Institute (a rather high-brow diplomatic mission of the Polish government), which struggled on their own to make a great impression.

In contrast, the influx of mostly young Poles into this country from 2004 has increased and invigorated the Polish

presence here. In many a town and city, there is now an equivalent to the Farnham Road in Slough. In some – including Slough itself – there is more than one such enclave. Go into Slough proper – the centre – and you will see more delis, some of them the size of small supermarkets. You will hear Polish voices everywhere, and see Polish signs. Go to other places where Poles have congregated in significant numbers – London, Birmingham, Manchester, Leeds, Southampton, Nottingham, Peterborough, Bedford, to name but a few – and it will be the same.

I suppose, really, we should not be surprised. Poles are famous for their ability to travel. The Polish diaspora is termed *Polonia*, which refers to the waves of Poles who emigrated from their homeland over the centuries, often fleeing persecution from invading forces or starvation – or simply looking for work. There are estimated to be a staggering 10 million Americans of Polish origin, including 1.5 million in the wider Chicago area alone.

The lesson of *Polonia* is that itinerant Poles have often ended up settling long-term in their chosen destinations. When one considers the delis and the hairdressers, the restaurants and the clubs, the newspapers, the success that Poles have made of work and school, the mortgages, and everything else that indicates opportunities seized with both hands in order to forge a way of life here, one thing becomes clear. The UK is no longer just a home from home for Poles. For many, it *is* home.

4 - Education, Education, Education

Influx of Polish children into schools has "helped improve British pupils' grades"

Mail Online

You may well have read the *Mail Online's* headline: *"Influx of Polish children into schools has 'helped improve British pupils' grades'"*. Apparently, the performance of Polish kids – especially in maths – has boosted standards amongst English pupils. Catholic schools, to which many Poles have sent their children, have benefitted in particular. And yet sometimes, it seems, this has been hard to take – or, at least, to adapt to – for British teachers.

Krystyna, a UK-based Polish friend of ours, tells an interesting story. Her daughter joined year 5 (i.e. at the age of around ten) at the local primary school, speaking very little English. Yet she performed superbly at maths. She did most of it in her head – as Polish children are encouraged to do – including utilisation of the bus stop division method where needed. Our teachers did not like this. "Write it down and show your working", they cried! "And don't use the bus stop method!" Confusingly, they at once rated Krystyna's daughter low *and* claimed she was already performing secondary

school level maths. It was rather like saying "you cannot be this good, and because we cannot see how you are doing it, there must be something fishy going on". Eventually, a common understanding was reached between Krystyna and the teachers – but many Polish parents have complained of similar experiences. UK schools, they say, do not sufficiently push their pupils. A 2010 study of the Poles' experience of schools in Scotland revealed precisely this, and that UK schools focus more on language than mathematical ability.

How can this be? Can Polish kids really outscore those of a G7 country, famed for its system of education? The answer is yes, and the reasons for it manifold.

Articles in the newspapers quoted a particular study at the London School of Economics (LSE). It suggested, inter alia, that the strong work ethic of immigrant Poles, and the high standard of schooling back in Poland, were reasons for the exceptional performance of Polish children.

So, for example, Polish education rates highly in OECD statistics. In their latest triennial PISA study (2013) – not a treatise on leaning towers, but rather the results of research into pupils' ability in reading, science and maths, with a particular focus on the latter – Poland ranks well above the UK, in 13th place. The UK languishes down at 26. Poland also well outscores the UK in science and reading. The last time the UK came close to Poland in the study was in 2006 (on that occasion honours were about even). The OECD comments on the 2013 report that Poland was one of nine countries to show a consistent improvement in maths performance in the period running up to the study (2009-2012), and one of just three countries to increase its share of top performers and reduce that of low performers. A recent reduction in the average class size in Poland, from 22 to 18, due to a demographic drop, has no doubt helped. We all know class sizes here in UK have long since been more around the 30 mark.

From where does this Polish prowess in education originate?

Most recently – since the Second World War – one of the good things (maybe the only good thing) the Communists did was to try to raise the level of education, and make it accessible to all, whatever their social class (of course the Communists were – theoretically – classless), and regardless of gender. No doubt they also had an agenda to utilise education as an ideological tool, but we can at least say most children did receive a good education, and that it would be unrealistic to claim Poland's excellent educational results of late have only reflected post-Communist reform (of which there has been plenty, as the Poles have restructured their education system several times in recent years). So, a good education in Poland has not been the preserve of the elite – as it has, to some extent, in the UK.

Further back in time, during the Second World War, Poland ran an entire underground state from London (read Jan Karski's astonishing account of this, and his adventures during the War, in *Story of a Secret State*). One aim was to keep the Polish language and culture alive during Nazi occupation (the Nazis saw Poles as slaves of a 1000 year Reich, and their way of life as dispensable). Some Polish pupils continued to study for exams at school and university level – but in secret. This shows the importance to Poles of their education. In the 150 years before the outbreak of the war, during most of which Poland did not exist as a state, having been partitioned by Prussia, Russia and Austria-Hungary, the Polish language (and, incidentally, the Catholic religion) were central to keeping alive the idea of a Polish nation. All in all, Poles have had plenty of historical reason to respect a good education; in such context, it is not such a surprise they have outperformed our own pupils in many cases. Nor, for that matter, is it surprising to hear Polish friends complain that British school teachers do not push their pupils hard enough, as the Scottish study suggested. Though it may also be right, as the LSE hints, that Poles who have made the effort to emigrate to another country are particularly motivated - both for themselves and their offspring.

When we moved to Buckinghamshire in 2007, we were lucky enough to encounter a grammar school system, and even more fortunate that our eldest daughter passed her 11+. So far she has discovered some Polish children in the grammar schools, though they represent a small minority. Competition for grammar school places is intense, and most parents employ a private tutor to boost their children's chances of success. This is not always easily accessible for immigrant Poles who are finding their feet and maybe not earning a great amount (tutors do not come cheap). And yet we know one Polish friend who employed a tutor for her eldest child in the year running up to the 11+. Another has three children, all of whom made it into the local grammar schools. The eldest won second prize in a national physics contest. My current Polish hairdresser started her son at a tuition centre at the age of six, but only to improve his English, not his maths. That's just as well. Being Polish, any further improvement in maths and he'd probably outshine the teacher.

We also discovered Saturday morning Polish language classes run by local Poles – at two different institutions. Again, there is an obvious enthusiasm to keep the language alive despite living in foreign surroundings. The classes are popular. My hairdresser will send her six-year-old to one of them from next year, she says, to ensure he gets a good grounding in Polish; he speaks more in English at present. In the meantime, because he reads voraciously everything in sight when in the bath, she pins up around him the trickier Polish consonant clusters. “Sz”, “cz”, “szcz”, “rz” and “trz” are now key accompaniments to his ablutions. Oh, and next year she may start him on Chinese lessons. Well, what the heck, he’s having lessons in most other languages! That child will be a polyglot before he knows it...

I think it is important that Polish classes have sprung up around the country. Children brought up in a country other than their parents’ all too quickly lose touch with their roots. Indeed, it becomes a badge of honour for them to speak the local language, and not that of their heritage. Our own kids are a case in point, although obviously the position is different in that they have only one Polish parent. We have not been able to get them to the local Polish classes on a Saturday morning, but Marzena makes up for this by speaking with them in Polish for parts of the day. They respond in English, of course – unless they’re trying to butter her up, when pidgin Polish is readily employed.

The influence on UK schools of the recent influx of Poles and others remains a controversial topic. The 2011 census revealed Polish has rocketed up the chart of foreign languages spoken by pupils, into fifth place, now sitting behind only (other than English) Punjabi, Urdu and Bengali.

Despite this, I don’t see any cause for panic, and wonder at the motives of those who do. Rather, I see things in straightforward terms. So, as regards integration, our schools need to make an effort to accommodate the immigrants, as well as vice versa. And many do. When my Polish brother-in-law and his wife came to the UK ten years ago, they sent their two daughters to the local Catholic primary school – a natural fit – which really tried hard. The teachers learnt for themselves a few basic Polish words. And they made Polish signs, to hang on toilet doors and in the canteen and so on. This is not kowtowing to a foreign culture – don't worry, English patriots: our nation will survive these small acts of kindness! – but it does help to make that awkward, initial experience at a new school (difficult enough in your own country) more bearable until the local language is learnt. After all, if Luton and Stansted airports can be plastered with signs in Polish, why not some of our schools? As if to prove the point, now, a decade after arriving in the UK, my nieces are fluent in English, which they speak with an accent a delightful mix of Southern Poland and North Yorkshire.

In terms of numbers, there will be increased pressure on class sizes – but the government must simply address this. Whilst we remain EU members and EU children arrive here, we must educate them, just as our own children receive education when they live abroad in the EU. It is no good scapegoating a people, especially their children, who happen to have taken advantage of an opportunity that has presented itself. As we have seen, it may even improve the overall standard of education in the UK, into the bargain.

5 - Family

It was around 2009, and we had been settled in Buckinghamshire for a couple of years. High time to do some work on our house (Marzena seems to have an unwritten rule no more than two years must pass between some sort of major building project, renovation, or at least redecoration). This time we fell somewhere between the latter two categories.

Krystyna, our aforementioned Polish friend, recommended a local Polish handyman whom she had hired before. It turns out it pays to know at least one local Pole when it comes to needing a recommendation, as they are well connected. Connection to a Polish cleaner is the best of all - they seem to know everything going on in the local community, something like the Matchmaker in *Fiddler on the Roof*.

Konrad duly turned up. He was two metres tall, lanky and ungainly – and one of the most pleasant individuals I had ever met. Always smiling and laughing, always wanting to please – Konrad has great charm, part of which lies in his unworldliness. I don't mean when it comes to his work, as Konrad is *Polak potrafi* personified. But – and I know it sounds incredible – Konrad will never, ever quote a price. I mean, before or after a job is done! Rather, at the end of a job, he says "pay me what you think it was worth". This reverse psychology is actually quite effective. Marzena and I have always paid towards the upper end of our own estimates, so nervous are we of offending Konrad.

Last time he did work for us, Konrad brought along his new work partner. Bartek looked half his height, and half his age. "Talk to Bartek when it comes to the money", he told us, wearing his usual infectious smile. "You know I don't do this very well!" But Bartek turned out only slightly more willing than Konrad to discuss money up front, and after the work was done, it was still left to Marzena and me to settle on a price. David Cameron's wonks at Number 10 would be proud, as this approach requires the art of "Nudge" – indirectly steering people toward your goal – to be exercised to its extreme!

But Konrad and Bartek's approach would work if we paid them twice what they were expecting, because of their incredible work ethic. For their last piece of work, they cleared away the moss that must have been gathering on our roof for decades. A locally-based firm had quoted over £1000 for the job, which would take around a week. "Don't worry", they told us, "it'll be done to a terrific standard – we'll even get up there and jet spray the tiles clean afterwards". Well, Konrad and Bartek did the job – including the jet spraying – in a *single day*; a day on which they arrived late in the morning having carried out a job for someone else beforehand, and went off late afternoon on their way to another job. We decided the price – as ever – and it wasn't £1000.

I mention Konrad because we have got to know him quite well over the years, during several jobs he has carried out for us. We soon learnt he has two partners in his private life – one former, one present – and children by each. The former he met in Poland; the present, once over here in the UK. Whilst this may not be the norm, it does tell us something of the pressures on those Poles who have emigrated to the UK, or come here for an extended period of time – sometimes leaving their immediate family behind.

I know from personal experience it is really tough holding down a long distance relationship, but it can be done. Marzena and I managed our first year and a half more or less apart. I also remember Jan, our very sympathetic landlord in Poland, when we lived there during the *Polska Dotty* days, telling us how, in Communist times, he had taken opportunities to work abroad for extended periods. On one such trip he did not see his wife and young son for two years! Their relationship survived, but it had not been easy.

Polish children dumped by parents heading for Britain

Mail Online

There does not seem to be much research on this, but Marzena and I know anecdotally of relationships that have come under strain due to time and distance spent apart. There was even an investigation in 2006 by – you guessed it – the *Mail Online,* claiming many Polish parents were dumping their children in care homes in Poland to take advantage of the UK's open borders. The stories investigated by the *Mail* – if you believe them – were horrifying. Apparently some teenagers in Poland took their own lives when their parents did not return for a long period.

I have no doubt there were some cases of this sort, but suspect they were at the extreme end (I also suspect the motives of the *Mail* in running this story so soon after Poland joined the EU). From my experience, it is more common for families to come to the UK together – a much more healthy option. Or, often, the husband/father arrives first in order to establish himself; in such cases it soon becomes clear that no amount of Skyping can make up for living apart, the family need to join him.

But I am equally in no doubt that the mass movement of a significant number of Poles to the UK has put severe strains not just on the emigrants, but also, like a ripple, on their families back home. Anyone who has read *Polska Dotty* will know the importance of the family unit in Poland, and therefore that any disruption to it is a serious matter.

On the other hand, this is only the latest wave of emigrating Poles. The Polish diaspora has seen many such waves, including twice in the nineteenth century, in reaction to persecution by occupying Tsarist forces following failed uprisings. Poland – a country of around 40 million people – will certainly survive the loss of 1 million or so Poles to the UK and other Western European countries, even if Polish governments vociferously bemoan the brain drain, and are forever thinking up campaigns to attract emigrants back home.

In my view, whilst emigration does undoubtedly place families under great strain, this latest exodus of Poles from their homeland may ultimately prove to be positive. We are talking as many as 2% of the population leaving the country. These Poles will either return to Poland for good, having earnt themselves some money whilst abroad, or settle abroad and return home from time to time on visits. There has been nothing like it since the mass displacement of Poles during and after the Second World War.

This process will, inevitably, bring fresh ideas into Poland. One of the first things many foreigners notice about the country, particularly if they stay for a while, is how homogenous it is - almost entirely white and Catholic. According to an early 2014 report by the EU's statistics body

Eurostat, it has the lowest proportion of foreign residents of any country in the EU (despite having taken in many Ukrainians since the Euromaidan protests and the change in that country's government). Now, Poland will not be able to avoid an influx of new thought, ironically from its own population outflow. For goodness sake, baked beans might become a staple meal in Poland! We'll see if I am right, at least about an injection of new ideas... if not the baked beans.

An interesting social phenomenon is the impact experiences of UK life may be having on relationships between Poles – even if they come here en famille. Both our cleaners have divorced their Polish husbands since coming to UK. And one said an interesting thing. She now has a new boyfriend – Polish, as it happens – but one who contributes around the house. Many Polish men are – how shall I put this? – *traditional*. That means they come home at the end of the day and expect a meal on the table. Now, many British men are like this, too (ask Marzena; she knows at least one) and I am sure this is also a generational thing. For example, I have noticed how the young chaps in my team at work are, almost to a man, more than willing to prepare a cordon bleu evening meal.

I bring up the rear, I am afraid, but even my eyes pop out at how some Polish wives will look after their hubbies (jealousy on my part, maybe). We know one who, going off herself to work all day, used to leave her husband a fully prepared lunch, covered by a plate warmer such as you would find in a canteen or hotel. It was like room service! He worked from home, so could easily have fended for himself. For many Polish women in the UK, this tradition of the all-embracing Polish mother/wife – Poles call it *Matka Polka,* something like the Jewish *balaboste* – will continue unabated and place no particular pressure on a relationship. For others, it may be the straw that breaks the camel's back, their *Shirley Valentine* moment. Incidentally, the indulged husband of whom I wrote a moment ago now prepares his own lunches.

For those Poles who come here still single, there may inevitably be cross-fertilisation of a different kind. I know of many Polish-British couples, for one thing because I have come across several reader reviews of my book along the lines "I bought *Polska Dotty* for my English (/Scottish/Welsh/Irish – take your pick) boyfriend. It's a great introduction for him to my culture". I say "boyfriend" because it does usually seem to work that way around. The legend of the Polish beauty lives on...

6 - Language

> **Revealed: The language map of England which shows where up to 40% of people say English is not their mother tongue**
> Mail Online

January 2013 – and one of those lurid tabloid moments that seem to have punctuated the Poles' experience here. First it was "There's half a million or more of them over here!" Then came "They're better at maths than us!" And now we read "Polish has become England's second language!" And, in fact, the third in UK after English and Welsh.

Some hack had spotted a story. But when this latest one came out, I remember thinking to myself, how much of a story? We already knew upward of a half a million Poles had entered the country. And – surprise, surprise – to a man, woman and child, they spoke Polish. That makes around half a million plus Polish speakers, with the Welsh-speaking population hovering at around 600,000. Do the maths, as they say. And sure enough, the headline derived from the 2011 population census, the results of which only came out in early 2013, taking time, as these things do.

The *Mail* – don't worry, I'm not expecting positive reviews from them – took their usual opportunity to score some points on the back of this revelation. They declared that only 13,000 Poles had been expected per year, that immigration from Poland was at its highest in 2007 (96,000), that nearly a quarter of UK-based Poles live in London, making up 2% of the capital's population, and that in Boston, Lincolnshire – where a row developed after historian Mary Beard said fears over immigration were a myth and public services could cope – roughly 1 in 20 inhabitants spoke Polish.

As usual, the prevalence of spoken Polish is patchy. So, the census revealed, Ealing had the highest proportion of Polish speakers, at 6% of the total population. Again, hardly a surprise as it had already become a mainstay of the Polish community in the UK, with former pilots and other Poles settling there after the war. The aforementioned Boston had the highest proportion of Polish and Central and Eastern European immigrants generally, hence the spat between Mary Beard and, as it turned out, a third generation Polish immigrant who was quoted as saying: "You go down to the high street and it's just like you're in a foreign country". Memories, it seems, can be short.

Polish: a crash course in England and Wales's third language

The Guardian

There has been a welcome philological exchange from this otherwise existential threat to our way of life (as the tabloids would have it). *The Guardian* entered into the spirit of things, offering "a crash course in England and Wales's third language". They translated into Polish ten choice phrases, beginning with "You don't happen to do a bit of plumbing do you?", followed by "Of course you don't, you're a neurosurgeon, I'm terribly sorry". *The Guardian* certainly got it; maybe Poles in the UK are not all neurosurgeons, but certainly one feature of recent Polish immigration has been highly overqualified Poles (yes, even doctors) serving behind bars and the like.

Inevitably, more and more English words have found their way into the Polish language – certainly into the language used by Poles over here. As I noted in *Polska Dotty*, Poles were never shy of utilising the odd English word, such as *karta kredytowa* for credit card, *monopolizacja* for monopolisation, and *gwarancja* for guarantee. Now, in business, Poles will slip words like "IT", "PR" and "marketing" into their conversation, often adding an incongruous declination at the end. *Dzial Marketingu* (Marketing Department) is an example. Apparently, Poles back in Poland are noticing this trend in their peripatetic kinfolk, and it even has a nickname: *Ponglish*.

When it comes to the language abilities of Poles in the UK, Marzena and I have noticed a difference according to type - though I would not say it's a revelation. It seems, roughly-speaking, to follow the level of a Pole's education and qualifications. So, neither of our cleaners have spoken English particularly well – the latest barely at all – though both have made up for this with their ferocious cleaning. It'll take you a day or two to find anything that was not securely put away before their visit. And of course, their connections in the local Polish community are legion.

One debate that has developed is how far Brits should help those Poles who are not proficient in English. It's really a microcosm of the whole multiculturalism debate. The trend, of course, is now away from multiculturalism and toward deeper integration. I am not opposed to this. It is well known there are elderly people in other immigrant communities in the UK who have been here a lifetime and still speak barely a word of English. I don't think that helps them, whatever impact it has on us. Equally, I don't think this will be a major issue with the Poles, most of whom speak English to a greater or lesser degree, and are relatively young, willing and able to learn or improve.

Plumbers, electricians, builders and the like are pretty damn good in English. I suppose it is difficult to carry out a significant piece of work for a customer – such as fitting a boiler – without being able to communicate in your customer's language. In any case, many Polish plumbers have qualified up locally, for gas (Gas Safe) and electrics (NICEIC), and you must, presumably, be competent in English to do that.

As for professional types, such as doctors and dentists – you can take it as read their English will be better than your own. But this is not to damn the hundreds of thousands of non-professional Poles working in bars, clubs, restaurants, and so on. Have you ever had trouble communicating with a Pole over here in English? I'll wager not.

Some Poles are themselves against special help, arguing it slows down their learning of English – but my view is it is beneficial to give reasonable assistance to immigrants. The signs put up for a while at my niece's school when she first came to the UK are a good example, as are the Polish language translations of local authority literature available around our way. How else can immigrants who do not speak English know their duties and exercise their rights? This does not threaten integration, or perpetuate a failed concept of multiculturalism (if you believe it has failed). It is, simply, right and proper. Having to understand basic English, for example, to become a British citizen – that may be a different story.

So, the Poles are generally proficient in English – or, at least, becoming so – but where will it end? Will they lose their Polish language? Never totally, of course. We have seen how much, traditionally, they value it. They have set up their own schools, in addition to those that were already run by the established Polish population in UK.

Anecdotally, I have noticed when we visit homes of Polish friends, they all speak Polish to each other. Recently, we went to a party at one such friend's place. It was attended mostly by Poles, but with the odd "foreign" spouse thrown in – a Czech Wife, a Mexican husband… and me, the token Brit! Though the Poles broke easily into English when chatting with non-Poles (even my broken Polish did not tempt them back to their mother tongue, which they no doubt feared I'd butcher some more if encouraged) – it was otherwise Polish which was the order of the day.

I suggest this will change. No amount of Saturday morning Polish classes will prevent the second generation of Polish immigrants speaking English at school, then at college, then at work – and with their friends. It's rather like my own great grandparents, who spoke Yiddish, to my own grandparents, who understood Yiddish and dropped into the sentence the odd, evocative Yiddish word, to my parents, who don't understand but are still fond of grabbing a piece of Yiddish where no English word will suffice - some *chutzpah* (cheek) here, a *szmata* (rag) there. In fact, for obvious historical reasons, this particular comparison is not so much "rather like" as exactly the same; *szmata* is a Polish word, too, with the same meaning.

I wonder how long it will take until, for some Poles, the only recognisable connection they will have with Poland will be their surname. A long time, maybe, but in the meantime, perhaps a thought to soothe poor Mr Farage's nerves...

7 - Health-care

Pole to Pole

BBC Radio 4

Around mid-2014 there was a half-hour programme on BBC Radio 4 about the Poles, entitled *Pole to Pole*. All features in the British media about Poles have to be entitled either *Pole to Pole,* or *Poles Apart*. By law. It's the only play on words they can think of. Admittedly, making a headline out of "poleaxed" might not prove too easy. A Pole loses a job, perchance?

Features in the mainstream British media about Poles settling in the UK since 2004 have punctuated their stay here regularly, if infrequently. They have not always been well done or accurate. I remember one beginning, errantly, "Since Poland became a member of the EU in 2007...".

But this particular one was better. Well-presented and humorous, it gave a solid impression of how far Poles have integrated into British society. One of the most intriguing moments came when the programme turned to address health-care. A Polish mother explained her child had become severely ill, and was having trouble breathing. She waited three hours in a hospital (she did well there, but probably doesn't know it), only to be told there was nothing wrong. It transpired the child had bronchitis, whereupon it was offered... ibuprofen. The mother explained that, in Poland, the child would have been offered at least three different types of antibiotic (wow!).

She's not wrong. Medical care in Poland is very, very different to our own. At least to our own medical care *now*. In the past in the UK, people of my generation will recall becoming ill as a child, and receiving a *home visit* from a GP. Yes! A home visit! Let me spell that for you: H-O-M-E V-I-S-I-T. At a home visit, if drugs were needed, the doctor would open up his briefcase – like something out of Inspector Gadget – and on most occasions present you with a drug there and then. Including antibiotics! *Antibiotics*. Shall I spell that for you?

Nowadays, of course, things are different. Even just to see a doctor – at their surgery, that is; doctors don't travel anymore, I think they get car sick or something – you must first negotiate the Ferocious Receptionist. This is an experience akin to those of Indiana Jones when, in his quest for treasure, he must avoid floors that drop away, spears that fire from nowhere, and a huge round boulder that chases him through a cave. In the case of the Ferocious Receptionist, the only way through to the doctor is to remember the secret password, which is "It's an Emergency, I'm Really Ill". If asked a second question – such as "What is wrong?", don't forget to have the name of a serious illness at your disposal. It's something like being a Mason.

Once in front of the GP, don't expect drugs unless you are, indeed, at death's door. To be fair, the authorities in this country are trying to counter a growing and dangerous resistance to antibiotics, which could one day kill us all. It just seems sometimes they've gone a bit far, and are willing to sacrifice a few of us in the meantime in pursuit of this greater goal. My own doctor, at least, tries to steer a middle line. During recent visits, he has penned me prescriptions for antibiotics but urged me to use them only if my symptoms persisted, murmuring as he writes about how they all get fined these days if they over-subscribe.

It is all very different in Poland. Poles won't mind my saying – they say it about themselves – that they are very... health conscious (I'm trying not to say a nation of hypochondriacs). This runs right through them. So, as noted in *Polska Dotty*, ask a Pole how they are and you won't fare much better than receiving the reply *tak sobie* (okay) – compared to the autopilot British response of "fine, how are you?"

Poles see a doctor regularly – I'd say their system of health-care is more preventative. As examples, Polish women are offered regular gynaecological check-ups (and complain they are not offered the same over here), Polish children are seen by paediatricians rather than GPs, and prospective employees in Poland are medically screened as part of their job application process. As for antibiotics, a Pole definitely goes to a doctor fully expecting to receive these, rather as we did in the past. The mantra amongst Poles over here – it was quoted on the radio programme – was that GPs only ever tell you to take paracetamol. We know of one Polish lady in our home town who was told by her GP (I don't know whether or not in good humour) "you Poles are demanding patients. You always wish to be referred to a specialist".

Well, maybe he was not wrong, but again – it's in the culture. Watch Polish TV and you will be amazed at the number of adverts dedicated to medical products (including an unfeasibly wide variety of creams). Venture out on the streets, and you will find a pharmacist on every street corner – usually modern and gleaming. And this commitment to health-care begins at an early age. In the UK, we are now used to every child having their own red book detailing their medical history. However, Marzena recalls a former work colleague from Poland telling her of when, years ago (during Communist times), she had been with her child in the UK. The child had needed medical help, and so the colleague had shown its red book to the doctors. They inspected it like it was moon rock. They had never seen anything like it! I myself don't remember having been the subject of any red book, and by the way my kids take an interest in theirs, I reckon I would have remembered.

One thing I have noticed – which makes it easier for Poles to access medical care – is that local surgeries in Poland seem to do more than over here. They are run more along the lines of the polyclinic concept the government is only now introducing in the UK. Also, dental care in Poland is generally of a high standard, and not as prohibitively expensive as in this country. That explains why many UK-based Poles save up their dental problems until their next trip back to Poland – and why many Brits indulge in "dental tourism", visiting Poland for more significant dental work such as implants.

This is not to say health-care in Poland is unbeatable. Yes, in certain areas, it is top drawer – treatment of certain cancers springs to mind – but day-to-day it certainly helps to have enough money to go privately. Affordability is not necessarily a problem. Unlike in the UK, where a few large players dominate the market – BUPA, AXA and so on – many consultants in Poland run small, private clinics, to subsidise their state salaries. The resultant high degree of competition forces prices down. The medics still do very nicely out of it; the patients receive quicker and usually better care.

This is precisely what the mother of the bronchial child featured on Radio 4's *Pole to Pole* show decided to do. At a not inconsiderable cost of £60 per visit, she went to one of the *Polish* doctors' surgeries springing up around the UK like mushrooms.

A good example of such private healthcare operating in the UK on Polish lines is Mr Medyk. Founded in 2008, it now has more than 50 staff. Its surgery is open seven days per week, until 11pm on most days. Appointment slots are for 30 minutes, at a cost of £70. It has tens of thousands of patients on its books including – and this is the particularly interesting bit – thousands of Brits. It seems I am not the only one harking back to a time when service was paramount.

The owner of Mr Medyk agrees, emphasising that patients receive a better service than on the NHS. He pedals the by now stereotypical Polish line that British GPs merely send you away with an instruction to take paracetamol. He also makes the point that Mr Medyk is cheaper than a private GP appointment at BUPA. Maybe, but £70 is still an awful lot of money for most – Brits or immigrant Poles.

However, the fact Mr Medyk and other private Polish doctors' surgeries are thriving is evidence enough that attitudes to the NHS among Poles in the UK (and some Brits too) are at best mixed. It is also evidence that, so far, the integration of Poles into the British way of life has only gone so far. Poles are not only visiting their own delis and hairdressers and restaurants and clubs, but even their own doctors. Mind you, you can't really blame them. If there is one thing about which we all wish to feel most at ease, it is our health.

Speaking of which, I feel a tickle of a cough coming on. Anyone got the phone number for Mr Medyk..?

8 - Politicisation

It is 2014-15 – general election time in UK. Immigration has become a main plank of the debate. In this day and age, immigration means an influx of EU economic migrants, which means an influx of Central and Eastern Europeans, which means...mostly an influx of Poles.

Interestingly, at no point during the election campaign did the debate become specifically anti-Polish. This did not surprise me. Surveys show the Brits who consider Poles have had a beneficial effect on the UK outnumber those who do not. Indeed the only negative result in polling about the Poles is that they have made an insufficient effort to integrate – something we shall explore in Part III when we talk to the All-Girl Polish Book Club.

There were vague attempts by the likes of Nigel Farage, leader of UKIP, to malign immigrants, if not Poles per se. On one memorable occasion, a few months before the election campaign proper, Mr Farage missed a paid engagement in Wales. He put down his tardiness to traffic on the M4, which, he said, was no longer as navigable as it used to be due to "open door immigration". He was widely pilloried for that comment, as well as (somewhat bizarrely) challenged to a duel by a Polish prince who is resident in the UK. Make no mistake, however, that there is a fierce, ongoing debate over immigration, especially from within the EU, and therefore, due to their sheer numbers, Poles are effectively at the centre of the storm.

It was not always like that.

Yes, back in the day, when I was growing up in the UK – in the 1970s – immigration was a topic for debate; its manifestation included openly racist TV shows such as *Till Death Us Do Part* (painful to watch now). Enoch Powell's infamous *Rivers of Blood* speech had only been made a few years earlier, in the late 1960s. But things changed, including the advent of political correctness, and for decades immigration was little discussed. Multiculturalism was the thing, nationalism a dirty word, and the Union Flag and Cross of St George became the preserves of extreme right wing political groups (and football fans). If you remember, Gordon Brown made rather cack-handed attempts to resurrect the flag, and British patriotism generally during the previous election campaign, with the slogan "British Jobs for British Workers".

I mention all this because I cannot help thinking that Poles and other Central and Eastern Europeans – who comprise the bulk of recent immigration – have been unlucky enough to arrive here just as immigration has returned to the mainstream political agenda. On the face of it, this was no coincidence. The opening of the floodgates from Central and Eastern Europe in 2004 provided an opportunity for the likes of UKIP to increase their influence and vote. But, in reality, UKIP – the main force rekindling the immigration debate – was around long before 2004 and the arrival of the Poles, railing initially against the Maastricht Treaty and Britain's membership of the EU generally. No doubt they saw – and still see – the arrival of a large number of EU economic migrants as an opportunity to rail further against the EU and in favour of their holy grail – withdrawal from it.

I therefore hope Poles reading this will realise – if they do not already - that, as well as being the focus of an immigration debate in the UK, they have also, to a degree, had the misfortune to get caught up in it.

So, have the Poles been more a force for good in this country than anything else, in particular in economic terms? According to the aforementioned surveys most Brits say yes, but steady sniping from noisy and sometimes noisome others mean this has become a hotly debated topic.

Polish invasion that's SAVED my home town

Mail Online

The odd thing for me is that the arguments and figures are overwhelmingly positive, and so it is difficult to find any genuine grounds for debate. So, we know that:

- Polish workers are extremely well-considered by employers
- They have contributed billions of pounds to the UK economy
- They have taken on undesirable low paid jobs, such as fruit-picking, without materially impacting wages for such low-skilled jobs
- But they are also, in general, more highly qualified than other migrants, and increasingly well-qualified
- They have settled in and revitalised run down areas of towns and cities (an example being parts of Southampton, where according to the leader of the

City Council, Poles have "been a breath of fresh air" to the city – as reported by the *Mail Online*)

- A significantly lower percentage of Poles take advantage of the benefits system, compared to the indigenous British population
- According to the 2011 census, they have the highest employment rate of any other group when analysed by birth (81%, compared to 69% of UK-born counterparts)
- According to the independent Office for Budget Responsibility (OBR), the current high net migration will add 0.6% to the potential output of the British economy and increase tax receipts rather than be a burden, as most migrants are of working age
- The OBR also opines that the recent rise in net inward migration has not led to widespread displacement of existing workers

Lies, damn lies and statistics, maybe – but it'll take a lot of lies, damn lies and statistics to make a cogent counter-argument and persuade me that – overall – Poles have not been a significant economic benefit to the UK. And, incidentally, to Sweden and Ireland, the other countries that allowed early Polish immigration. Is it just a coincidence that the economies of these three nations have fared better, on average, than those who initially shut their doors to the Poles?

Regarding benefits, a Polish assistant I met recently in one of the stores in the Bicester Village outlet shopping centre put it well. She said she came to the UK eight years ago, with no job. But she did not dream of taking benefits, and lived initially off her savings. Within two months, she was in work, and had been ever since. She was doubtful any restricted access to the benefits system for EU migrants – as has been proposed – would deter Poles, because they came to work. Her comments typify those of most Poles with whom I speak on the subject.

Of course, such a large influx of EU migrants has caused problems, in particular, pressure on public services. Many also argue wages were forced downwards and, contrary to what the OBR has stated, existing jobs, especially those traditionally taken by low-skilled school leavers, were impacted. There are arguments too that Poles have repatriated much of their money to Poland.

Some of this may be true, but the positive economic case for the recent wave of immigrants from Poland and elsewhere seems overwhelming. We may simply have to face up to the fact that, as the figures show, inward migration has helped our economy to flourish, and may well continue to do so in the future. The fall out on public services will just have to be addressed (by, incidentally, one of the richest countries in the world, which arguably should have invested more in its public services long before Poles and others migrated here...).

I know some reading this will not be persuaded. For some, no amount of statistics will convince them that the arrival of the Poles and others has been a good thing. I confess to having little sympathy for such people's views, but I do have a great interest in their motivation.

In *Polska Dotty* I tell the story of when Marzena and I were on a train in Kazimierz-Dolny, eastern Poland. I won't repeat it here, but the outcome was that a Pole we met, when challenged by me about his apparent anti-Semitism, squirmed and explained he didn't really dislike Jews. It was the *blacks* he couldn't stand.

Whilst I would not wish to tar everyone with the same brush, I have little doubt there is a constituency within the anti-immigration movement in the UK who would not want the Poles or any other Johnny Foreigner type entering the country. That is the true explanation for their opposition to Polish and other immigration, where raw statistics do not support their argument. If you wish to know the sort of person I am talking about, he is a maudlin former colleague of mine who made it his business to visit every far flung corner of the diminishing British Empire before it was handed back. I remember a trip he made to Hong Kong, and even to Macau (a former Portuguese colony). He was a fair bit older than me, and I suspect he is now retired and manning a battlement in Gibraltar.

Marzena tells an amusing story of taking the train home one day from London to Bucks. This particular train was headed for Bicester Village, and much of it was filled with Chinese tourists. But what was irritating the man sitting next to Marzena was a couple opposite, evidently from Spain. The man turned to Marzena. He told her he'd been living around these parts for ten years now, and every year the number of foreigners – he cast a disapproving eye in front of him, and then spat it out - like the *French* couple opposite - had grown and grown. It was beyond belief, he said. What did *she* think?

Marzena replied to the sophisticate that it was of no concern to her, and he'd find the couple opposite were Spanish. She replied, as she would, in her Polish accent. He – in a rare moment of genius – noted her foreign accent and asked Marzena where she was from. She told him, whereupon he said something complimentary about the Poles – and that it was the forthcoming invasion of *Romanians* and *Bulgarians* he was worried about.

Well, it was the man in Poland all over again. Jews, blacks, Chinese, Spanish, French, Romanians, Bulgarians… I fear there are some out there who just need someone to hate.

The comedian Stewart Lee performs a hilarious satire on UKIP, including a short but brilliantly observed vignette on UKIP's attitude toward the Poles. The context is UKIP complaining vehemently about all the immigrants who have come to the UK over the millennia, the most recent example, of course, being the Poles. *"Bloody Poles"*, exclaims Lee, "Coming over here, being all *Polish* and mending everything... fixing all the stuff we've broken, and are too illiterate to read the instructions for... and doing it better than us - in a second language. *Bloody Poles.*"

Many Poles are beginning to feel stigmatised and scapegoated. Now, we should not lose perspective in all this. Poles have integrated remarkably well into British life, they like it here, and are well liked. But I sense this insidious criticism of them is beginning to take its toll.

In February 2014, Polish groups in the UK protested by publishing an open letter to David Cameron and other UK political leaders. Their beef was against anti-Polish discrimination. The month before, a Polish cyclist had been attacked by a group of thugs who recognised his nationality from the Polish flag on his helmet. They allegedly shouted xenophobic abuse, and physically attacked him. Coincidentally or not, in the same month David Cameron had remarked that Poles were taking advantage of the UK's benefits system. Would he have said the same of others in the UK who, unlike most of the Poles, wield a vote?

In the summer of 2015, some Poles in the UK attempted to organise a strike to highlight what they brought to the UK economy. In truth, it was a well-intentioned but ill-conceived affair. At the headline demonstration in Parliament Square, journalists were said to outnumber demonstrators (some wag suggested all the Poles were at work...). On the same day, other Poles gave blood to show their solidarity –

though even this was criticised as politicisation of a worthy cause. The main result of all this, so far as I can see, is that Poles have inadvertently stigmatised themselves, which is a shame. Google "Poles in the UK" to this day, and the main results are all about the failed strike – good publicity for it, but surely not the main impression Poles wish to give of their life over here.

The basic position of many Poles is that they feel they work hard, and contribute much to the British economy and wider society – but that this is not recognised. I suspect Poles also feel their voice is not heard in the democratic process, which may partly account for why so many say they will apply for British citizenship.

We have touched on this question – but what, precisely, is the Polish contribution to wider British society, beyond the economic? As noted, the impression on the locals is that integration is the one area in which Poles may have fallen down – but is that a fair assessment?

I see some truth in it. As I have mentioned, much of the world the Poles have built for themselves in the UK is inward looking – to serve their own compatriots, be that in food, or hairdressing services or medical care, or even (as we shall see shortly) supply of building materials and labour. I have to say that – for my part – this is not a problem, and seems only natural. My Jewish ancestors settled in places such as London's East End, before foraging further afield, and to this day there are large communities of other ethnic groups in particular parts of the country – for example, the Pakistani community in Bradford. Further, Poles are very welcoming. When I see Brits in Polish delis or other establishments, there is never a hint they are not welcome. Why should they be? They are customers, after all!

I think the locals need to chill out a bit, and not feel so threatened. Any group will inevitably set up its own infrastructure to cater for its own needs. As long as this is not done in a discriminatory way, then I don't see a problem. In time, there will be more intermingling – especially when word gets out about those Polish doughnuts...

In any case, Poles and Brits inevitably mix a lot. In jobs, when accessing public services, in relationships, as friends. This is a dynamic process, and, as noted, subsequent generations of Polish immigrants will undoubtedly assimilate.

It may be that, in the meantime, Poles should make a bit of an extra effort to integrate – for example, getting involved in local politics, or taking British citizenship to make their vote count. But then, in some areas, they are already doing so, and have been for a good while.

For example, only two or three years after Poland joined the EU, several newspapers reported that the "Polish invasion" had swelled the numbers attending Catholic churches in this country. Having seen their population of worshippers dwindle along with those of most organised religions in the UK, the Catholic Church suddenly received an unexpected boost when hordes of devout Polish Catholics arrived.

The Poles are more devout than the Brits, of that there can be no doubt – and are a different *kind* of devout. We have already seen how Catholicism helped keep the Polish nation alive when Poland went off the map between 1795 and 1918, and in living memory the Church supported the *Solidarity* political movement to overcome Communism. Thus has the Catholic religion become a part of the fabric of Polish society. According to an *Economist* report published on Christmas Day 2015, Poles attend church on a monthly basis in far greater numbers than the people of any other European country. As many as one half of recent Polish immigrants to the UK are said to be churchgoers (probably a greater proportion even than in Poland). The number of Polish masses being held has increased, sometimes to as many as seven times a day in a single church – and the churches are often packed out.

> **Devout Poles show Britain how to keep the faith**
>
> The Guardian

As far back as 2006, the UK Catholic hierarchy recognised the opportunity with which it had been presented, with the Catholic Church in Scotland declaring an increase in numbers of 50,000, according to the *Guardian*. Eight years later, in 2014, the same newspaper reported mass Christian migration from Central and Eastern Europe had slowed the decline in church membership, which would now not be evident until 2025 (having been anticipated to begin in 2020). Good news for the Catholic Church in the UK – although the fact such a large influx of worshippers has done no more than slow the decline shows the challenge the Church faces.

> **Church attendance has been propped up by immigrants, says study**
>
> The Guardian

It has to be said, even in this sphere, that Poles have been accused of failing to integrate sufficiently. Cardinal Cormac Murphy-O'Connor, head of the Catholic Church in the

UK, apparently declaimed the Polish migrants who were "creating a separate church in Britain" (to which the Poles might have replied "Um, Henry VIII, anyone?").

It seems the Poles cannot win.

I consider the Poles are doing just fine in their level of integration in the UK, and are already more integrated than other minorities in this country who did not, perhaps, arrive with the same broad compatibilities - historical, political, cultural and religious, to name but a few.

That said, we know ghettoisation can be a dangerous thing – something that breeds misunderstanding and worse. My advice to UK-based Poles would be, if they can consciously find room to make that extra little effort to integrate into UK society – perhaps in some way they would not otherwise think of – then all well and good. After all, as *Polska Dotty* readers will recall, a lack of integration is one thing I cannot be accused of during my stay in Poland!

Equally, as I have mentioned, Brits should do their best to make life easier for Poles and other immigrants. Integration is a two way street. We saw this in the way the local school treated my Polish nieces, writing signs for them in their mother tongue. I have visited other schools where, clearly, the class has been asked to familiarise itself with Polish culture because there are Polish-themed drawings on the walls.

Or, why not begin even earlier, at the border? Returning from a family holiday recently, my eagle-eyed eldest daughter noticed the immigration officer had written down eye colours in Polish - *niebieski* (blue), *zielony* (green), *brazowy* (brown), and so on. He kept the sheet on his desk, all but hidden below the counter. We weren't entirely sure why. Something to do with the automatic passport machines, we surmised. Either that, or he was looking for a Polish bride...

Part II - Home Extension

(A Tragicomedy in Five Acts)

Dramatis Personae

Jonathan – A homeowner

Marzena – A homeowner, and Jonathan's wife

Big Mick – A budowniczy (builder)

George the Cat – Big Mick's sidekick

Bogdan – A young murarz (brickie)

Piotr – An old murarz

Dawid – A young hydraulik (plumber)

Arek – Dawid's assistant

Andrzej – An old plumber

A supporting cast of thousands of peripatetic Polish labourers and suppliers

Scene

A home on a suburban street in Buckinghamshire

Act 1 - The Bargain

Big Mick the builder came recommended. By Elene – the Georgian mother of a pupil in our eldest daughter's class. Marzena – and, for that matter, I – somehow gravitated toward the Central and Eastern European parents at the school gate. There was some sort of affinity between us. Big Mick – a Polish builder – had done some work on Elene's house. A small extension. It had gone pretty well, though costs had escalated. Don't they always, on building work? You only need to watch the endless number of TV shows on the subject...

Big Mick is not *so* big. A little over six feet, I would have said, but he is well-built, and with a slight barrel-chest he looks imposing. He would always describe himself as Mick, his name in English – to make it easier for Brits to pronounce, he told us – and somehow, the local building suppliers had dubbed him Big Mick. He has a full head of wispy brown hair, dimple cheeks, and – most noticeable of all – hangdog eyes. His natural expression seems to ask: "You're kidding me, aren't you?" This can be most disconcerting.

For the major extension we were planning, we invited several builders to quote. Mostly Polish, but also one English, and one Polish-English cooperative. The English builder quoted a small fortune compared to most of the Polish builders – although one Polish builder was nearly up there with him. This was a well-established Polish builder who worked on properties in Kensington, mostly. It would not take forever before good Polish builders, who built a reputation, began to charge similar to their English counterparts, Marzena and I mused. This one did not get the job.

But Big Mick did. We wanted a builder who not only quoted a keen price, but also seemed an honest sort. Battered by building horror stories related to us by friends, family, and the TV, we determined to engage someone with whom we hoped we could hold a decent conversation even when things turned difficult on the job, as we surmised they inevitably would.

Big Mick was calm and polite at our first meeting. He was also already beginning to make helpful suggestions as to how we might conduct the work. And he seemed to be a hard worker. After we had decided to appoint him, but before we had contracted with him, a two-metre triangular pit had needed digging in our garden to ascertain whether or not the roots of our large beech tree stretched to the area where the extension was to be built. The tree was under a Tree Preservation Order (TPO) meaning its protection was now a priority over all life as we know it in the UK. Apart from animals. Animals are somewhere up there with trees in the psyche of the British establishment.

Big Mick came around one day with a Polish worker – an old fella' who, in all honesty, looked past his sell by date. But he and Big Mick proceeded energetically to hack away with pick axes at the difficult Chiltern chalk – and within no time at all had dug a good pit, about 18 inches deep. No small feat. The price for doing this was reasonable. "That's it," Marzena and I determined, "this is the builder for us".

The main job was not insignificant. Our house – which sits on a typically steep Chiltern hill on the edge of town – was to be extended to one side. Reaching back the full depth of the house. And up two storeys. After years of threatening, Marzena finally had THE BIG PROJECT into which she had been wishing to sink her teeth. In the preceding couple of years, there had not been a single dinner-time during which the subject had not been raised – the number of additional rooms there would be, the configuration of the rooms, the type of furniture to be fitted – and so on. Even I was quite relieved when this phoney war drew to an end, and the beginning of the real work was in sight; it also meant the end to our monothematic dinner-time conversation.

So, four metres out to one side of the house, eight metres (the depth of the existing house) back, and two storeys up. That would be the extension. 64 square metres of floor space in total. Downstairs, the additional space would tack onto an existing room of exactly the same size – our kitchen-cum-dining-room-cum-living-room, where we spent most of our time. The new room would fulfil the same functions, but be twice the size – eight metres square. Open plan, Marzena assured me, was how everyone lived these days. We were practically troglodytes not to have done it already. Upstairs, our pokey master bedroom would be extended, and an additional bedroom with en-suite bathroom created.

And all to be built into a steep garden that surrounded the existing structure, meaning it would be necessary to gouge out large amounts of earth and hold back what remained with new retaining walls. The test pit Big Mick and his worker had dug would be a mere pock mark in comparison.

Our surveyor – a feckless sort whose work would later cause both Big Mick and us plenty of angst – eventually managed to produce extension plans that achieved both planning permission and building regulation consent. The potential TPO minefield was navigated – though not before the local authority had added a meaningless "barrier" condition to the planning permission, which would add an unnecessary extra cost (here, as we shall see, Big Mick would come into his own to mitigate our loss, as the embodiment of *Polak potrafi*, the Pole who can do).

All of which meant it was time to sign a contract with Big Mick for the job. Marzena had actually been against it. "Polish builders aren't used to a contract," she explained to me. She was right, of course, and I knew it. But I also knew that Elene's much smaller extension had greatly bust its budget – particularly on materials - and we could not afford the same. This project would really stretch us, and so the price had to be the price – bar unexpected problems or additional work, for which Big Mick would need to be fairly rewarded.

I picked a simple, standard building contract, but - sure enough - Big Mick was nervous to sign even this. So I talked him through it, explaining there were options to be selected and blanks to be filled in, covering what the work would comprise, how long it would take, for how long it would be guaranteed, and so on. There was no doubt Big Mick was suspicious. He knew I was a lawyer, and clearly thought we were trying to fleece him. In vain did I explain contracts did not have to be one-sided, and could be drawn up to cover the middle ground – a compromise for both parties – right from the first draft. Instead, Big Mick had his adult daughter, who spoke excellent English, read the contract, and he brought her around on one occasion as we discussed contract issues.

But eventually Big Mick signed up. In spite of his concerns, we'd held a number of amicable meetings with him at our house, some attended by his wife as well as his daughter. There seemed to be a mutual respect, and of course critical to this was the fact Marzena was Polish, and so could speak with Big Mick and his family in their own language, both literally and culturally. Indeed, this was advantageous both ways. Over the years, during minor works to our existing and previous homes, I had noticed how much more attuned Polish workers were to Marzena's way of thinking. In particular, the importance of cosmetics – the final look and style of the work. In contrast, Marzena had found herself at odds with many British workers – who did not have as much of a discerning eye. It boded well to be having this, the most sizeable project of all, carried out by Poles.

We did need to overcome one impasse, which was that Big Mick did not wish to guarantee the price of the materials he supplied – only the labour. He could not control the former, he explained. With Elene's experience still fresh in our minds, we insisted, and a compromise was reached. Big Mick would include materials in the price, but with a mark-up on his previous quote to cater for potential price rises. It seemed fair enough, and would come to stand us in good stead as the job progressed.

And so the bargain was struck, and the date set. On 31 March 2014, Big Mick and team would break the ground, and work would begin on the Great Lipman Family Home Extension. Oh, and it'd all be completed four months later, by the end of July.

Act 2 - An Unwelcome Surprise

Things began exceptionally well. For a start, the weather was unseasonably dry. In such auspicious conditions, Big Mick and his men arrived on time that first day and got straight into it – and from the start, Polish pragmatism was at the fore.

Due to the slope of the terrain, the side of our garden onto which the extension would be built sits a good metre and a half or more above the drive, atop high retaining walls. So, the men built a wooden ramp up to it. The ramp was somewhat Heath Robinson – or the Polish equivalent. Plywood was joined end to end using batons, and then the whole thing lain from the drive up to the garden, at an angle of about 25 degrees. Big Mick gingerly tested it when climbing up for the first time, and then – once it was decided everything was ok - that was it! No holds barred. In the ensuing weeks, diggers and cement-mixers, as well as human traffic, mounted and descended that ramp as if it were made of reinforced concrete. The original structure was still standing at the end of the entire job, although by then the plywood was splitting, and you could walk only on one side because the other had warped and fallen away to the ground. We warned many a foolhardy building inspector to take care when using that ramp (on the basis we wanted them alive, and able to grant us a completion certificate).

Some of the first materials to be carried up the ramp were a large number of further plywood boards, and batons. These Big Mick – and his right-hand man, George the Cat – utilised to create THE BARRIER, which stood comparison to the Berlin Wall. It was the condition that had been inserted into the planning permission to protect the beech tree subject to the TPO. It seemed to make no difference to the authorities – or the tree specialist we were forced to instruct at our own expense, pursuant to the planning permission condition – that the tree sat 10 metres down our steep garden from the extension, meaning its roots, extensive as they must have been, would have stretched down the hill, away from where the work was to be carried out. Neither did it seem relevant that the trial pit dug in the corner of the extension footprint closest to where the tree stood had revealed only miniscule tree roots. No, none of that mattered. What mattered was that we had to build a replica of the Berlin Wall on top of the grass, along the full length of our garden, so that building materials could not be deposited on the far side, nearest to the tree. Some may say the council wished to be seen to be doing something to protect the tree, and to keep the local arboriculture trade in business – but I couldn't possible comment...

Big Mick and George the Cat assembled another ramp of plywood, 20 metres long, which was erected on its side to form a fence. A clever system of wooden supports kept the whole construction upright. It did the trick, and passed the scrutiny of the arboriculturalist on one of his many (expensive) trips out to us to check the precious tree was still standing. On the ground, more plywood was laid adjacent to the Wall on the extension side – another requirement specified in the planning permission. The whole thing, in the end, came to around £1000 – something for which we had not budgeted. We were £1000 down before we had even begun. But had the protective wall and path been built to the precise British Standards specified in the planning permission – looking like something at the side of major motorway work, with a path covered with layer upon layer of impact-reducing materials – the price would have been double. We had Big Mick to thank for this, and, to be fair, an arboriculturalist who... could see the wood for the trees, and approved the final outcome.

We also had George the Cat to thank. George – Jerzy in Polish – was not *actually* a cat, I hasten to add. But he might well have been. He was diminutive, but wiry and springy. He could turn his hand to almost anything – more even than Big Mick – and fit into spaces no human had the right to. He was also forever having near misses, falling from a ladder or roof, cutting himself with a saw or nail. And yet he always seemed in control (and was always smiling). It was for these reasons we gave him his feline sobriquet.

Big Mick and George the Cat were constantly joined by a veritable cast of itinerant Polish workers. Evidently, the days when you had to visit the shop next to the Polish centre in Hammersmith, London, in the hope of finding some available Polish workers who had advertised on the Wailing Wall, were long gone. It was clear Big Mick had established a local support network of workers with building experience, as well as plumbers and electricians to help him with the trickier specialist work. This was evidently possible because so many Poles had entered the UK.

There was something of a hierarchy among the workers. At the top sat Big Mick, closely followed by George the Cat. Later, a first *murarz* (brickie) Bogdan, followed by a second, Piotr – who it turned out was the old man who had helped dig the TPO trial pit – were engaged to build the walls. As semi-skilled workers, they sat somewhere in the middle of Big Mick's pyramid. Next came tilers and painters, and at the bottom a stream of Polish general labourers – those who helped dig the ground, for example, who came and went like the seasons.

Talking with these various workers – as Marzena and I would try to do – was social research in itself. It gave us a snapshot of the sorts of Poles coming into UK – their backgrounds and their ambitions. They were, almost to a man – and they were all men – hard-working, friendly and articulate. I remember one, who was only on site for a week or two, telling us his regular job was room service at a Heathrow Terminal 5 hotel. But this opportunity with Big Mick had turned up, paying more, and – take note, politicians – because he was on a zero hours contract with the hotel, he had taken the opportunity to come and work at our place. He had been in the UK for seven years, was married to a Polish woman in the UK, and had put his university IT studies on hold (for a long time, evidently) whilst he earned some money. He was not sure whether he wanted to settle in the UK or Poland. I felt a bit sorry for him. If he really was studying IT, and if he really had put his studies on hold for so long, I wondered if he would ever return to them. I suppose he was not the only young Pole facing such a dilemma.

Marzena also chatted with the workers, evidently much more fluently than me. In contrast to the loquacious room service/IT specialist I had met, she also remembers a young Pole who came one day to assist with some digging. I remember him too - young, but already balding, he resembled the old man who Benny Hill used to slap on the head at regular intervals. On his day on site, he sidled up to Marzena, and asked, apparently sincerely:

"Where am I?"

Marzena was slightly taken aback, but answered with the name of our town.

"Never heard of it", he replied, deadpan, before returning to his work.

He was gone by the next day – maybe to some other place he'd never heard of.

So, the ramp and tree protection were in place, the weather set fair, and a crew had been assembled – even if some of them didn't know where they were. Things were ready to proceed, and proceed they did. Big Mick and his team got off to a fast start.

They dug the foundations for the extension which, allowing for a walkway that would run around the walls, extended well beyond eight metres by four metres. This meant they had to remove a hexagonal patio that sat to the side of the house. It was solidly built, and due to the slope, perched on thick concrete on one side, but Big Mick and his men had it in the skip in no time at all. To help them, they hired a small digger, and George the Cat could be seen operating its arm with a broad grin on his face. He used it not just to attack the patio, but also to remove vast quantities of soil. A friend of mine had always joked we lived on the North face of the Eiger. It seemed his comparison was not far wrong.

The upshot was that the first skip was filled in no time at all. Big Mick noted this, and it was the first sign of things beginning to go awry. At this rate, he would need more skips than he had reckoned. Skip = Cost. Many Skips = Big Cost. Big Mick was worried about the Big Cost.

His solution was to panel the ends and sides of the skip with unwanted plywood boards that extended above the walls of the skip itself. Effectively, Big Mick had manufactured a bigger skip, into which he would funnel as much waste material as possible. When this expanded skip looked full to overflowing, Big Mick would then wave in George the Cat, who would drive his digger along a narrow board onto the top of the skip and force down the detritus inside with the digger arm.

The skip suppliers – as most of Big Mick's suppliers – were Polish. They were called "Polskip". Every Polish supplier

Big Mick found Polonised their name by adding the prefix "Pol". Not exactly world-beating brand creation, but at least you knew where you stood. And Big Mick knew where *he* stood. He argued vociferously with the Polskip driver who picked up the first skip – loaded to the gunnels as if Big Mick were trying to smuggle out the Lost Treasure of Captain Kidd – who argued the lorry might struggle to mount the skip as it was so overloaded. But the skip went on the lorry – Big Mick practically taking the controls from the ingénue skip lorry driver, and none of the subsequent drivers seemed to worry. Either they were used to overloaded skips, or word had got around that Big Mick was not to be messed with.

Nevertheless, as the work progressed, I could not help but feel there was some plot afoot at Polskip to get their revenge on Big Mick. Skips were never collected and replaced on time, and on occasion we would be delivered a skip whose floor was coming away. Big Mick would tear his hair out. On other occasions, the skip would be deposited at the foot of our drive, some five to ten metres from where it needed to be, at the top, near to the extension work. Big Mick and team would then set to work, slipping narrow round scaffolding polls at each end of the skip, and rolling it – *uphill* – into position. It was awkward to say the least. But Polskip were a half to two thirds the price of any other skip firm on the market, and so up with the gremlins Big Mick had to put. For our part, Marzena and I were amazed at the price differential, and the network the Polish building trade had established in UK. Clearly, it was – amongst other things – thanks to knowledge of cheap Polish suppliers, that builders such as Big Mick were able to undercut the established building trade. All the same, we wondered if the latter had not been profiteering these last however many years.

In these early days, everyone was highly impressed with Big Mick and his team. Our neighbours opposite – one of whom was of Polish origin, and knew about the Polish work ethic – asked if we could confirm they were Polish, which we did.

"I knew it!" she exclaimed. But even she could not believe their commitment. A typical day lasted from around 7am to 7pm. They also worked Saturdays, though slightly shorter hours. Sundays were not unheard of if the job demanded it, nor were bank holidays. They were also exceptionally neat and tidy, though this fell away somewhat toward the end of the job, as the challenges increased and the job became less economical for them. In those early days, though, they could not do enough. On one occasion, in the first week or two, water mixed with concrete washed down from our drive into the road. It looked dirty, and would not have made a good impression on the neighbours so soon into the job. Perhaps sensing this, Big Mick and his men sprayed the road with our pressure washer and brushed away the stubborn remains, working late into the evening. By the time they had finished it was pitch dark, and they were searching around with torches for any parts they may have missed. No wonder the neighbours were impressed.

At the start of that late night clean up, Big Mick had asked me if I had a pressure washer in my possession. I had, as it turned out – an old one of my father's that had seen better days, and that I had not used for a while. We plugged it in, and soon realised we would need to connect it to an additional length of hosepipe so the sprayer would reach to the road. But we did not have the right connector. Big Mick quickly fashioned a connection by splitting one end of a hosepipe, pushing it onto the sprayer, and fastening the whole thing using a hose clip. Before carrying on with the spraying, he then put me right on the missing connector piece.

"They don't sell them in UK," he told me. "Here, they prefer to sell you an expensive length of pipe than a cheap connector". He looked at me with those hang-dog eyes, expecting a challenge or an answer – but I didn't have either. I later discovered he was right. The particular connector we needed did not seem to be readily available on the UK market.

This became a theme of Big Mick's work: how things were often better in Poland. It is not an uncommon theme amongst Poles over here, as I know from half a lifetime spent with Marzena. So, these particular hosepipe connectors were not available in UK; tile-cutters were overpriced over here, and not as effective as those sold in Poland; and – the piece de resistance – almost every item we purchased ourselves for the extension: kitchen furniture, a bathroom suite, windows, railings – to name but a few – Big Mick could import for us from Poland at the same price *in zloty*. That is, five times cheaper. Through a combination of not wishing to delay the work, and sheer disbelief, we never took Big Mick up on his offer, to his apparent disappointment. He would shrug his shoulders on each refusal of this kind, as if to say "it's your funeral".

And then there came an unwelcome surprise. One day, Big Mick happened to glance at our copy of the detailed building regulation drawings – council approved – and noticed two one metre square boxes marked at each end of the extension. On closer inspection, it transpired our surveyor had proposed two one metre square holes be dug – *three metres in depth* – to ensure the integrity of the extension. But he had only added this requirement in a later draft of the drawings, and only provided us with one copy. All our other drafts – including the one from which Big Mick was working – excluded it.

In the end, whatever the whys and wherefores, the additional pits needed to be dug. Three metres down. Into solid chalk. Big Mick and his men set to work, and in less than a week, had managed it. They slaved away, during a particularly hot spell of weather. Sweat poured from them. At one point, George the Cat could be seen scooping out earth using the mini-digger as it all but disappeared into one of the two additional holes, fellow workers seated on its rear to counterbalance the weight. He was still smiling. But Big Mick less so. If he had known about the additional foundations, he told us, he would have hired a digger with a longer arm.

When the digging was finally over, a vast quantity of concrete was poured into each pit. What with the concrete and the additional labour, Marzena and I found ourselves a few thousand pounds further outside our budget – but again we were fortunate that Big Mick had stepped up to the challenge. We had lost only a week or so, and were still within our project contingency monies – though they were running out fast.

There were some perturbing moments at this early stage of the project, and bizarrely they all seemed to centre around the skips that came and went with alacrity (despite the best efforts of Polskip to slow things down). As well as Big Mick's alarm at the number of skips that it was likely the job would require, we had our own concerns. We noticed that impressions were being made on our tarmac drive where the skip lorries' hydraulic feet pushed down to support the lifting process. And a drain cover in the drive, sturdy though it was, was becoming increasingly bent by the comings and goings of heavy vehicles. These things were hardly noticeable to Big Mick. On one occasion, I got nervous about the hot exhaust fumes from our boiler, which were feeding directly onto thin waste boards protruding from the skip. It wasn't out of the question that those boards would catch alight. The next day, Big Mick obliged by cutting away some of the boards with a circular saw. He was willing to allay my fears, but he was not going to move that skip until it was well and truly packed.

But all in all, we could not complain – and nor could Big Mick. The additional foundation work had been unexpected, but we had paid him for all of it. Bar the extra skips he was likely to need, supply of which came within his total quote to us and so irked him – every penny Big Mick had to spend on materials above his own estimate really irked him – things looked reasonably on track, both in terms of cost and timing.

And beyond that, a good rapport had developed. Marzena enjoyed having people around to chat with in Polish every day. When it came to describing what she wanted on any particular aspect of the extension, her taste matched that of the workers. It seemed Polish taste was best. This augured well for the more cosmetic aspects of the project to come, such as fitting the kitchen, which Big Mick's team would also do. For their part, the Polish workers were very self-contained. When we were at work, they made their own tea and coffee. And when we were at home, they left us plenty of space. In fact, so much so, that we began to wonder where they... did their business. Big Mick had been amused to note in the building contract how an over-zealous draftsman had graciously stated the workers were allowed use of our bathroom facilities during their time on site. Yet Big Mick and his crew never seemed to take up the offer. For a while I thought the local MacDonald's facilities must be getting good use. Then, after the building work was over, I noticed that, despite the disruption – the dust and rubble and concrete, the diggers and wheelbarrows and cement-mixers criss-crossing our garden and flattening the earth and plants – the shrubbery in one corner of it had grown particularly well during the period...

Act 3 - Walls Come Tumbling Up

Bogdan was cherub-faced and of quiet disposition. He was also a great brickie. I don't think Big Mick and he had worked together much before, and by the end I suspected they would not do so again. Big Mick and George the Cat seemed a tad ambivalent about Bogdan. Not because he did anything wrong. But he did not have their tough, no nonsense approach. At one point he fell off a ladder, landing on his wrist, which swelled quite badly. He sat in our garden tending it. I was quite concerned, and gave him ibuprofen. As it happened, the wrist got better quite quickly, and Big Mick and George the Cat had a *told you so* look about them.

But Marzena and I liked Bogdan, and it was down to him the walls of the extension went up at a good speed, and evenly. His attention to detail was second to none. On one corner of the extension, a porthole window needed to be put in to match an existing one on the other side of the house. Bogdan copied it to perfection, cutting bricks in half and then shaping their shorter ends into curves so the window was offset by an elegant half brick circle. He did something similar at the edge of the roof gable, layering roof tiles flat and stepped onto one another – again precisely to match the effect on the existing structure. There was no question this had to be done, he explained to us. We again put this down to a Polish sense of the aesthetic. A British builder who quoted us for the extension had explained it would be additional cost to mirror the porthole window; in other words, it was optional whether or not we did it.

Funnily enough, of all the troubles we had with the extension, it was the bricks that nearly drove Big Mick to distraction. They were brown rather than a standard red, and difficult to get hold of. They were also more expensive than standard bricks. Big Mick knew this when he took on the work, of course, and had priced accordingly. But somehow his calculations had again gone wrong, or the price of these bricks had escalated, or they were no longer available – or some such. So anxious did Big Mick become over these menacing brown bricks that at one point – breaking our vow not to pay Big Mick extra for what he had promised us in the contract – we dipped into our pockets to assist in the purchase of some more of them. It was either that or have a very unhappy Big Mick on our hands.

On one occasion, bricks managed to confound us all. Not the brown variety, this time. It began when Marzena phoned me at work to explain we urgently needed "TCP" bricks. These conversations at distance were wont to cause problems. Big Mick would say something to Marzena in Polish. She would phone me at work, and we'd speak in

English, as we usually do. And the whole thing would go pear-shaped from there. It was better when we were all together on site. Then, if there were ever a Polish word for which he did not know the English translation – and Big Mick's English was pretty good – he would whip out his phone and dive into a Polish-English app. But we were not all together, and Marzena was asking me if it would be acceptable cosmetically for the first three to four bricks in the extension, from the ground, up to be "TCP" bricks. *Well, they wouldn't become infected,* I thought to myself. Eventually, the mystery was solved, and *DPC* (damp proof course) bricks were duly installed at the foot of the extension walls. Still, I couldn't really blame Marzena for the misunderstanding. Plumbing work, including radiators – *kaloryfery* in Polish – were to become a theme of the building project, and I spent most of its duration describing them as *kalafiory* (cauliflowers).

The miniature Polish world which we now seemed to inhabit continued to be responsible for our extension as it arose around us. A Polish firm erected scaffolding when it became impossible for Bogdan to go any higher on a stepladder (or, at least, any higher without falling off again). Polish skip lorries continued to reverse into our drive, and continued to mangle our drain cover in the process. An unending flow of Polish workers came and went. Some of them even knew which town they were in. Through it all, Big Mick ruled firmly, if not quite with a rod of iron. He lost his cool from time to time, when the workers made mistakes and he would threaten to dock their pay. I never knew if he carried out this threat. I suspect not, as in his heart of hearts Big Mick probably knew – as the boss – he bore some responsibility for whatever had gone wrong. In any case, in time, he would calm down, relations would sweeten, and all would be well again.

The truth is Big Mick was a knowledgeable builder, practical, an imaginative problem-solver, and always looking to the bigger picture – but not always the best organised. From time to time he would exhort us to purchase materials – the windows, patio tiles – as if our lives depended on our doing so at that very moment. Said purchases would then sit in the garden gathering dirt whilst, for whatever reason, it proved impossible to fit them at the anticipated moment.

Big Mick would also repair to Poland from time to time. We understood this – he had responsibilities back home, including his own property – but inevitably, work would slow when he was away, if not come to a halt, and mistakes would be made.

But it was impossible to question the work ethic of Big Mick and his team. It is true that, on occasion, especially as the job went way over schedule, we would encourage Big Mick to send more workers on site – without much success. For a day or two an extra worker would be spotted, never to be seen again afterwards. However, workers turned up almost every day, and continued with their very long hours – sometimes until nine or ten pm – as well as working on the occasional bank holiday. By the end of the job, we had one neighbour complaining (not unreasonably) that such noise on a Saturday morning or bank holiday was too much to bear, and another asking for the builders' telephone numbers because never in their lives had they observed such a committed workforce...

The walls of the extension were now two storeys high, and so the time came to knock through the eight metre outside wall of the old kitchen/dining/living area. The process itself went smoothly. I came home from work one day, and there it was – the lower part of the wall had gone, and the building above was now held up by a series of steel supports. At last, downstairs, we could see the entirety of the large living space we had designed – albeit roofless – and begin to dream of how it might look when finished.

If we thought the period up until work began on the extension had been a phoney war, we rapidly came to understand that – despite the disruption of skips and workers and noise and a whole lot more – in reality, the phoney war had only just ended. Now that the extension had connected with the original house, bringing with it the dirt and dust, we retreated more or less into one room upstairs and one downstairs, in each case on the side of the house furthest from the works. Downstairs we occupied the lounge, along with an overflow of furniture from the kitchen and hall. We "cooked" with a microwave, and had a toaster and kettle at our disposal. That was it. The local Chinese takeaway was to do very well out of us in the ensuing months. Upstairs, Marzena and our two girls slept in one bedroom, I on a narrow futon in the adjacent study.

Nevertheless, life (and the building work) continued relatively smoothly until, a short while after the bottom half of the outside wall had been removed, we noticed huge cracks in the remaining top half. Also, on the "good" side of the house, furthest from the extension, doors which had for years closed perfectly well began not to do so anymore. We noticed all this in the course of one evening, and quite panicked about it. Was the house about to collapse? We phoned Big Mick, who told us not to worry; he'd take a look in the morning. We phoned family members who knew more than us about physics, and they were not quite so confident. What to do? It was late, but I made the fateful decision to take the children to my parents for the night, 45 minutes' drive away. Marzena remained behind.

The decision was fateful not because anything untoward happened – the building did not collapse on Marzena – but because of the impact it had on Big Mick. He was highly sensitive to the impression others had of his work. Though his English was not the best, he knew the expression "cowboy builder", and was forever explaining to us that he wasn't one. It was almost as if he resented having to fight a stereotype that immigrant builders were shoddy. We knew Big Mick was not a cowboy – and told him so – but when faced one evening with a home held up by a few steel supports, mighty cracks in the wall, and a builder who said he would be around to inspect only the next day – we had simply taken precautions. As it turned out, Big Mick was right. By cracking, the upper outside wall was simply doing what upper outside walls do when no longer fully supported beneath. It was due to come down soon, anyway. As for the badly fitting doors, that was likely to be the house settling as major construction was carried out on it.

The work went on. A colossal, eight metre beam was installed at ceiling height downstairs to support the new structure, which finally allowed the upper part of the misbehaving wall to be demolished. Problem solved - no more wall, so no more cracks. The installation of the beam was not without its problems. Big Mick had to adapt our surveyor's drawings, which necessitated an additional visit from the building inspector to approve the change. It transpired our surveyor had planned for the beam to show beneath the ceiling line, and for it to be cut in two and then welded back together. "Never heard about anything like this in Poland", Big Mick had muttered, before finding a solution with which the inspectors were happy. The result was the beam did not need cutting, and was hidden in the ceiling. A job well done.

Fitting the roof was next, and – once again – we would have to rely on Big Mick and his men first to spot difficulties in our surveyor's approach, and then to resolve them. On this occasion, Big Mick took off existing roof struts – the main gable needed to be opened up and doubled in height – that should not have been removed. *According to the drawings.* But when the inspector came to visit, he agreed there was no other way to do it, the implication being that our surveyor had asked us to make an omelette without cracking an egg. Worse was to come. Big Mick's team mounted a couple of new metal beams high up at roof level – only to discover one end of each would poke slightly out of the roofline! It transpired the beams needed cutting at the ends to match the angle of the roof. Our surveyor suggested this was a mere detail – the sort of adjustment builders needed to make as they went along. *Some adjustment*. The two weighty beams had to be taken back to ground level, and a local welding firm called out to sheer the metal off – blowing what remained of our contingency monies in the process. Had the surveyor planned for angled crank beams in the first place, none of this would have been necessary.

We had the impression our surveyor was experienced in books and designs, but not the real world. This would figure if his rare visits to us were the norm, because he would not have found himself on site often enough to gain better understanding of a job's practicalities. We were miffed as he only lived locally and had promised to be on site regularly. But Big Mick was a calming influence, and it was interesting to get his take on things. He asked if we had paid the surveyor in full. We had. "Well, then," he opined, with the equanimity of a man who was not, ultimately responsible for the additional cost of transforming normal beams into crank beams, "there is nothing to be done." Big Mick explained he would never have paid the surveyor up front in full. "It wouldn't happen in Poland", I interjected before he could do so, receiving an affirmatory nod in response.

Taken together with other mishaps, such as the two additional concrete pillars we'd had to incorporate into the foundations, these structural problems slowed the work down significantly, and increased the cost. But they were not uncommon for a large building project – and underscored the ingenuity of Big Mick and his gang, as well as their strong work ethic. Indeed, if it had not been for the plumbing fun and games that were to come, all in all we could have counted ourselves lucky and called the project a reasonably smooth ride.

With the roof and walls in place, the extension began to take shape and become recognisable as a living space. A floor was put in upstairs, and partition walls to create the bedrooms and en-suite bathrooms. Downstairs, in the large space, Bogdan worked on the fireplace, which was supposed to be an inglenook affair. In fact, Big Mick did not seem overly familiar with the inglenook concept, and so we ended up with a veritable tongue-twister: a half in half out hearth – in other words, half inglenook, half open. It all stemmed from the fact Bogdan built the hearth out from the wall - not into it, and closer to the chimney. As a result, the escape flue needed to run horizontally a short distance from the back of the log-burner to the chimney in the wall, apparently not an ideal set up. But some judicious last minute research on my part revealed that as long as there was more vertical than horizontal in the route up which smoke escaped – and outside was a mighty two-storey high vertical chimney – the draw should be adequate. And it was. Big Mick was also not cognisant of the UK's Hearth Regulations, and it was only thanks to some further research on my part that we ended up with a size of hearth that met the legal requirements.

Bogdan was extremely diligent (slow, Big Mick called it) and insisted the effect be first class. True Polish aestheticism, we decided. And sure enough, the result was spectacular - a beautifully laid fireplace of decorative bricks (red with a swathe of black), topped by a thick, pagoda shaped wooden beam. It actually was from an old pagoda. Big Mick had kindly visited a local timber yard with us, spotted the beam, and negotiated the price down on our behalf. We appreciated his hands on and helpful approach, and from the quotes we had received from local builders – who itemised every item they might have to source or task to which they might have to lift a finger – convinced ourselves this sort of assistance was an advantage of "going Polish".

When the fireplace was complete, Big Mick and Bogdan stood looking at it, hands on hips, and asking for our opinion. They took pride in their work, and naturally enough wanted some appreciation – and we were effusive in our praise. The quality of workmanship deserved it. But as the job went on, and ran further and further beyond the timetable and budget – Big Mick's and ours – necessitating a more hurried approach, this would become a harder and harder circle to square. Big Mick still wanted the praise; we wanted him to maintain the standard that merited it.

The fireplace completed, Bogdan was gone. He apparently had another job to go to. We wondered if that was the full story. A building project is an intensive experience, and we sensed tension between Big Mick and Bogdan. Maybe it was about the pace of work, maybe something else. For our part, we were sorry to see him go, but happy to see the return of Piotr, the older individual who had helped Big Mick build the experimental tree pit.

Piotr was a factotum... of sorts – and also a character. He had a strange way with him. Asked a question such as "will it be necessary to add temporary valves whilst work is done on the water system?", he would reply, in a drawl, and with a smile on his face that looked like a combination of disbelief and reassurance, "Ye-ees, it will be necessary to add temporary valves! Spokojnie [calm down] – it will be necessary... ye-ees". It was a bit unsettling at first, but we got used to his style, and ability to reply to us with nothing more than a regurgitation of the same words and concepts we had put to him in the first place.

In fact, Piotr's was an unfortunate story, and I suspect this was the reason he did not wish to rock any boat of any kind – including by saying anything that could in any way be interpreted as contradicting any view held by Big Mick, the hand that fed him. He confided in us he had run a successful business in Poland, but – like many prosperous older Poles – lost his fortune in the shock economic therapy introduced in the late 1980s by Finance Minister Balcerowicz. This was an attempt rapidly to transform Poland from a communist economy to a capitalist market economy. The Balcerowicz plan was successful, but in the short-term many Poles lost their jobs. Piotr had to sell everything he owned, and his wife had told him from then on he would only work for others. He rented a room in a family home in the UK, he told us, at £50 per week. I think his wife lived back in Poland.

Piotr's prowess was there for all to see. He could lay bricks, plaster, wire, plumb – you name it. *Polak potrafi*. Big Mick would often consult him. But Big Mick would also grow impatient with him. On one occasion he wired a large part of the kitchen incorrectly. On another, he was asked to connect a pipe extension to the main water supply to feed a new fridge we had bought, which produced ice and cold water. Once the fridge arrived, a plumber Big Mick had called in duly plumbed in the fridge at the back, but no water was forthcoming. The plumber went back behind the fridge, disconnected it, and blew down the pipe extension Piotr had fitted. In another part of the kitchen, near the sink, where the pipe extension should have connected, a trumpet sound could be heard. Piotr had forgotten to join the extension of pipe to the main water supply. For a moment, we wondered if it had really been Balcerowicz who had destroyed Piotr's business...

But all in all, Piotr was very much a credit to the team, in particular plastering and plastering the many extension walls, often until late into the evening, sweat pouring from his brow. We felt rather sorry for Piotr, and as Big Mick vented his spleen at him for his latest mistake, Marzena and I would ensure he had enough to drink, and was not about to keel over from dehydration or overwork.

With Big Mick, there were despairing episodes, episodes at which one had to laugh – and others that were a combination of the two.

Some of these were not of his own making. So, Big Mick fitted many of the window frames the wrong way around – but in accordance with the instructions on the frames. The Polish window supplier – recommended by Big Mick himself – had placed the "this way around" stickers... the wrong way around. Coming on top of the fact the supplier had been obliged to reorder most of the window frames, which it had measured wrongly – the firm had hardly covered itself in glory. However, this firm was part of Big Mick's network of Polish suppliers, and perhaps thanks to that – and, maybe, some choice words from me – we did end up with windows that fitted (the right way around), looked good, and were very reasonably priced.

On the other hand, Big Mick fitted a back kitchen door from the same supplier, and boldly declared it opened the wrong way. Given our experience to date with the supplier, I was inclined to believe Big Mick, but decided to take a look myself. I did so, and discovered Big Mick had fitted the door upside down.

On another occasion, Big Mick was adding wiring to our landing, which had been extended five metres or so to provide access to the new bedrooms. The landing was now quite long, and evidently necessitated several light switches. But, Big Mick demurred, it was impossible to fit more than two light switches on one landing line.

"Impossible," he said. "Nowhere in the world does a landing have more than two light switches."

"Nowhere in the world?" I asked.

"Nowhere in the world", Big Mick replied.

Big Mick looked at me with those hang dog eyes, imploring me to accept his proposition, or to pull a rabbit out of a hat. I pictured endlessly long hotel corridors punctuated by numerous red-lit switches to allow guests to punch on the corridor light on exiting their room; I pictured similar corridors on cruise ships with similar arrangements. But all I said to Big Mick, was "We already have four light switches for the landing".

Big Mick looked at me, poker faced other than for a hint of a smile at each corner of his mouth. Still staring at me, he called out, "George!"

George appeared from nowhere.

"How many switches are there for the landing?"

George seemed to know, but glanced around to be sure.

"Four", he replied.

"Piotr!" Big Mick bellowed.

Piotr appeared.

"Is it possible to have more than two switches for a landing light?"

"Of course!" Piotr replied, initially a smile on his face, and then a frown as he realised he might have landed his master in it.

"There you go, Mick", I said to him, "we'll have the first landing with four light switches in the *entire world*!" I patted him on the back as I walked off.

I suspect Big Mick was well aware there could be more than two switches on a landing light circuit, and the explanation for his approach was a simple and understandable need to shorten an increasingly unprofitable job. In fact, Big Mick – like Piotr – was capable in most aspects of the work. For example, as well as the structural side of things, he carried out most of the plumbing and electrical work himself. He also tiled one of the bathrooms. Later he would fit the kitchen, lay an outside patio, and weld and fit railings to new retaining walls.

"How did you learn to plumb and wire, and everything else?" I asked Big Mick one day.

"At school and college", he answered, "and learning on the job, including in the UK".

"Polak potrafi", I nodded, with a wink and a smile. A Pole can do.

"Polak potrafi what?" Big Mick asked, genuinely puzzled.

"Polak potrafi… everything", I tried to explain, implying the ability of many Poles to fix many things was a boon – but I could not have got it more wrong.

Big Mick enlightened me. This ability meant there was less work about in Poland for people like Big Mick. Poles came home of an evening and did their *own* fixing. It was better in the UK, Big Mick said, where people earned enough money to pay others to fix things for them. It reminded me of the Stewart Lee parody, "bloody Poles, coming over here, being all Polish and mending everything… fixing all the stuff we've broken". I countered to Big Mick it was impressive so many Poles knew how to fix things. *Wszedzie lepiej gdzie nas nie ma*, he told me. The grass is always greener on the other side. I think it was his way of disagreeing with me.

Big Mick and I would chat quite a bit like this. One time, he told me the Polish brain drain concerned him, without seeming to acknowledge he might be part of it. Not that he was content with everything over here. In a building context, pull cords in bathrooms perplexed him (why not switches?) – as did minimum heights for plugs and maximum heights for light switches. Outside of the building arena, travel was also a hot topic. Rather like the UK-based Polish IT consultant who wrote a *Random stuff that baffles me as an immigrant* blog one night and woke up to more than 1800 comments, Big Mick was bemused by our road etiquette. He asked me once why English drivers didn't indicate and whether it was true that there was no need to indicate when turning left. I had answers for these, but not his final query: "Why is my new TomTom worse than my old one?"

Big Mick was extremely money conscious – not a surprise for a builder – but had taken a discrepancy in pricing in this country to an almost moralistic level. So, it was criminal that work gloves for sale at £1.50 in Wickes were priced at £6.50 in Travis Perkins. Homebase was another culprit. One day I mentioned to Big Mick I had taken advantage of a 15% discount day there.

"Sure," he opined, "off prices that are 30% higher in the first place!"

I began hiding my Homebase purchases. Not that Big Mick was wrong about this. Marzena and I had long since noted a pricing hierarchy in DIY stores, as in most sectors, with Homebase somewhere near the top, and B&Q keenest of all. Big Mick's attitude just surprised us because a) this is the way of the world, and b) in Poland, of all places, there is a gulf between shop prices and those at *gieldas* – informal street markets where goods are cheerful... and cheap. But Big Mick and I usually found a way to end the conversation in accord.

"I did once buy a £40 Xmas tree for £3 at Homebase", he confided, coyly, evidently torn between the attractive price and an admission he had all but sold his soul to the devil.

I leave the last word on this subject to Big Mick himself. On one occasion, I owed him just under £150 for some materials he had purchased for the building work, which were outside the contract scope. I duly paid him the cash – £150 in notes – whereupon he began fiddling for the 12p I had overpaid.

"Don't worry about it!" I told him – but he would not be dissuaded.

He found the 12p, and deposited it in my hand.

"Money is money", he told me, with only half a smile on his lips.

He was not wrong.

Act 4 - Raining in My Dining-Room (Reprise)

Progress on our extension reminded me of the song *Dem Bones*. The two concrete pits supported the... *foundations* – the foundations supported the... *side walls* – the side walls supported the... *metal beams* – the beams supported the... *tiled roof* – Now hear the word of the... *builder*. And, they were all done. In addition, not only were there floors in on both levels, but the plumbing and electrics were well underway, as was the plastering and even some painting.

Perhaps bolstered by all this, Big Mick announced he was going on holiday at the end of the week. Fair enough, you might think, given the progress. But it was now the middle of September. We had been living, essentially, in two rooms for several months, and even in these – as all over the house – dust covered everything that didn't move (and even things that did). Big Mick had been due to finish the whole project by the end of July, so every day that stretched beyond that seemed a trial.

Nevertheless, Big Mick needed a break, we surmised. He had not been in the best mood of late. Maybe a break would provide him the impetus to finish the job swiftly on his return.

"Just one thing", we asked him, when he had explained that everything was on course and therefore he was going away for a couple of weeks. "What about fitting the new boiler and water tank?"

Big Mick regarded us with that by now classic look of disbelief.

"Ohhh", he touched his forehead. He had genuinely forgotten. "Don't worry. Moment."

He went off to make some calls, and then came to explain. His usual plumber was unavailable. But he had secured the services of Dawid, who would complete the job on Saturday and Sunday. Most of it would be done on the Saturday, when Big Mick would be around finishing off bits and pieces of work before his holiday (he was due to fly early on the Sunday morning).

It is fair to say Marzena and I felt uneasy about this at the time. It seemed a rush for such a major piece of work, squeezing it in before Big Mick went away. Plus, why had he completed all the pipework in the extension itself, and then plastered and painted over some of it, and lain the wooden floor throughout the kitchen over the rest of it – before having the boiler and tank fitted in the garage? Wouldn't it be more usual to test the boiler, tank and new pipework together, before covering it all up? But by now the job had run on so long, with so much still to do – fitting the kitchen, landscaping the garden and so on – that Big Mick wanted to get on, and we did not wish to slow things down.

Dawid came round early that Saturday. He was youngish – maybe 30 – stubbly, and shaven headed. He spoke excellent English, and was polite. He explained he was registered with Gas Safe (formerly CORGI), and showed us his card. He brought with him an assistant – Arek.

They worked apace, and as promised, by the end of Saturday, the boiler was installed. We were also promised the water tank would be in the next day. It was evening by this time, and having finished what he could, Big Mick bade us farewell and headed home. He hadn't even packed, he told us, as if to make us feel guilty. He was feeling the pressure of the project, undoubtedly. We hoped, next time we saw him, he would be refreshed. As it turned out, he wouldn't be – but then, we were to see him only a couple of hours later...

Not long after Big Mick had left, I popped down our outside front steps to the garage below, to look in on progress. No-one there. Strange. Even if they were not working, Dawid and Arek were usually to be found chain smoking in front of the garage. I went back up the steps, through the front door, and saw before me in the extension... the Statue of Liberty. Well, not actually the Statue of Liberty, but it looked not unlike. Arek was perched on one leg, the other stretched out behind him like a ballet dancer. This enabled him to raise one arm above him as high as possible. Clasped in the hand of his outstretched arm was the stubby plastic end of a vacuum cleaner, the metal wand having been dispensed with. Into the stubby plastic tube was being sucked... water! To the strains of the vacuum cleaner, a stream of water was making its way down the tube. It was emanating from the narrow opening above one of our freshly fitted lights. Elsewhere, in smaller quantities, more water was dripping from our freshly painted downstairs ceiling onto our freshly fitted (and expensive) wooden floor. Meantime, Dawid was running around like a meerkat, stopping stock still every now and then apparently to see what he could hear or spot. *We had a leak.*

I was especially sensitive to leaks, following the incident with Szymon many years earlier in our house in Pinner. There is something decidedly shocking in seeing water appear where it should not in your home – your sanctuary. This feeling, I can tell you, is intensified when it happens to you for a second time. Nevertheless – like a true Samaritan – my first thought was for Arek, the Statue of Liberty. Was it safe for him to be putting an electric vacuum cleaner in the path of a water leak?

But Arek was unconcerned, so attention turned to The Hunt for the Leak. The problem was, only Big Mick, and possibly George the Cat, knew where the pipework had been fitted. Because they had covered it all up, we needed their intelligence so as not to cause more damage to the floorboards and plaster and paint than was necessary. Big Mick – who by now must have been dreaming of snorkelling or sailing or Roman remains, or whatever he intended to do in Croatia where he was headed – to his credit, came straight back. Only it would take him a little while, he said, the traffic heading into and out of London (where he lived) that Saturday night was awful.

He duly arrived an hour or more later, and stormed into the house, ready for action and clearly agitated. Dawid had long since turned off the main water supply, but the downstairs extension was like a scene from the Bible. There was water everywhere, despite our efforts to mop things up with towels and electric hoovers. All we needed to complete the picture was an Ark – and perhaps a pair of real meerkats.

"Do you have a boat?" Big Mick asked. We didn't appreciate his humour.

Like a dentist faced with a particularly tricky patient, out came the tools. Unlike a dentist, the tool in this case was a circular saw. Big Mick and George the Cat went upstairs to our now extended master bedroom. They discussed something sotto voce – presumably debating the best place to make an incision – and then began cutting away at our newly-laid, planks of floorboard. Once done, they looked at what they could see, and George the Cat also groped around on all sides of the new hole with his arm, as far as he could reach. Nothing. More circular sawing. Again, nothing. Eventually, after several attempts – by which time our bedroom floor resembled a rotten jetty – the leaky joint was found.

"I didn't connect it right", Big Mick admitted with disarming honesty.

He stayed whilst Dawid switched back on the water, then ordered George the Cat to make a quick repair to our bedroom floor, so our bed could at least rest on terra firma – and then they were both gone.

Big Mick did return from holiday refreshed. He whipped his team into shape, and we began to see a pinch of light at the end of the tunnel. The two en-suite bathrooms – work on which had begun before Big Mick's holiday – were completed, and work began on the kitchen, before they moved to the outside.

Tiling and installing wooden flooring are Polish strengths – like many continentals (and now me, a convert) they prefer these to carpets. In Poland it is practically against the law to carpet your bathroom ("what is the point in that? It gets wet!"). Despite this, Marzena's preference in one of the en-suites – white tiles with blue grout in between and blue tiles with white grout – nearly drove Big Mick to distraction. It was not what he wanted at the tail end of a difficult project, but he got it done, and the effect was so stunning we now refer to this bathroom as the Sistine Chapel.

We jumped these hurdles, and others, with a touch of Polish derring-do into the bargain. One of the last jobs on the list was fitting fascia just below the roof line, including to part of the existing structure. George the Cat, using up one of his nine lives, had to beat a hasty retreat when he discovered the old, asbestos fascia which was being replaced housed a wasps' nest. I came home that evening, and – ever a twinkle in his eye – George took a long stick and beckoned me to the upstairs landing. From there, it was a metre and a half or so to the piece of fascia in question. George opened the transom window on the landing, and carefully began to push the stick out of it in the direction of the nest, part of which was exposed beneath broken fascia.

"Er, are you sure this will be okay, George?" I asked tentatively. I was nervous more of the nest than the asbestos. I feared George might be about to give the former a gentle tap.

A wink from George. "Don't waaary", he said, in his thick Polish accent.

A split second later, he gave the nest such an almighty poke with the stick – right into its guts – that bits of it fell away. He then withdrew the stick like lightning and slammed the transom shut. A swarm of wasps shot out of the nest in a number that should not by rights have fitted into it. A Tardis nest. I stepped back in fright. Fortunately, the window held good. And, within a minute or two, most of the swarm had gone back into the nest, leaving only a few straggling guards to drift rather aimlessly outside. George grinned with satisfaction throughout the whole exercise.

I called in a wasp controller who shot a copious quantity of powder into the nest, remarking it was strange how badly damaged it was. Never mind, he said, it meant the wasps would die quicker – probably within 24 hours. I didn't tell the man about George, who I was sure had broken some animal protection law or other. But I did text him a couple of days later to thank him for attending to us so quickly, and also for returning the very next day, when I was at work, to remove the nest. The controller texted me back, saying it was no problem... but that *he* hadn't removed the nest. I reckoned I knew who had.

The folks who came and went continued to surprise, disappoint and impress in equal measure. Dawid, it transpired, had fitted the hot water tank when he was not qualified to do so, making a mistake on a safety escape pipe in the process. We had to call in our regular, English plumber to rectify the situation. He was less than impressed at the standard of workmanship. On the other hand, Big Mick's regular plumber Andrzej (Andrew) became available, and attended the job to assist with radiators that were only half heating up in the extension. He seemed very experienced and capable, and improved the radiators. He was also, evidently, pleased to be in the UK.

"I voted for Poland to join the EU," he told us proudly, "and as soon as it did, I jumped on a bus here. I had only £10 in my pocket, and knew only one word of English – Slough."

To his credit, Andrzej now ran his own business with a couple of employees, and owned his home. He fitted my identikit notion of a Pole from the new wave of immigrants who had really established himself here – one who had arrived shortly after Poland joined the EU, and had, by a decade or so later, found success.

We were really, nearly there, when lightning – which isn't supposed to strike even twice – decided to make a third visit. I had got up for work one day and was brushing my teeth and washing, thinking how pleasant it was to be carrying out my ablutions in a beautifully tiled, finished en-suite bathroom that was part of a pretty much completed extension – when I shut the mixer tap off in full flow.

Thud!

What was that?

By now beyond sensitive and well on the way to paranoid I thought the noise sounded suspiciously... watery. I rushed around upstairs to check no-one was running a tap or taking a shower – but nothing. I hurried downstairs, still bleary-eyed, and although I could not see anything the heavy showering sound continued. Was it raining outside? I peeled back the curtain to look. No. Then, out of the corner of my eye, I spotted something. Water was beginning to leak through a light fitting (aka drainage route for dodgy plumbing) above the corner of the fireplace hearth. The flow increased before my eyes as I continued to watch, disbelieving. Coming to my senses, I bolted down to the garage to switch off the main stopcock...

Big Mick and George the Cat turned up, with Dawid in tow. They walked from one side of the kitchen to the other, avoiding piles of towels that were soaking up pools of water, mostly beneath light fittings. Out came Big Mick's circular saw. This time, he seemed pretty confident about where to make an incision. And he was right first time. In the ceiling above the corner of the fireplace, where the leak had first appeared, a plastic connector had apparently failed. You could see Big Mick was genuinely disappointed and perplexed by this rupture. Despite the job becoming more difficult for him, he had not skimped on plumbing supplies, buying good quality plastic pipes and connectors. He asked Dawid if he could explain the breakage – but he could not.

Marzena and I, though no plumbers, concluded Big Mick's plumbing problems – *our* plumbing problems – were a combination of bad luck and self-infliction. The latest leak appeared to be bad luck – a defective joint. But Big Mick, by his own admission, had made one bad connection on plastic fittings that need a good snap together. He also rushed to fit the boiler and water tank, testing them on pipework that had already been installed and covered over. Into this perfect storm – or adding to it – stepped Dawid who made one or two questionable decisions, including not installing a valve to reduce the high mains water pressure to a more manageable one. This latest leak was, maybe, an accident waiting to happen.

And these things *do* happen in building work. After each flood, some friend or family member or other would wax lyrical to us about *their* flood or *their* leak when they were undergoing building work. I just couldn't help thinking that, if this were a leak competition, Marzena and I were beginning to look like the "winners".

And then it was over. Despite the tree protection fandango, marauding skips, unexpectedly costly foundations, roof issues, a half-in half-out fireplace, ill-fitting windows, world-record breaking corridor light switches, half-heating radiators, incessant dust, delays, and leaks (mustn't forget the leaks!) it was really and truly - finally – over. Despite the differences of opinion and tensions – it was with heartfelt appreciation that we handed Big Mick and George the Cat thank you cards with a little extra for their troubles. I even had Marzena translate for them "All's Well that End's Well". She had to think about it, but eventually produced a meaningful translation. Big Mick quickly understood, and a smile tugged at each corner of his mouth.

I suspect, in the nicest possible way, we were each of us thinking: at last, we are free of the other!

It was just before Christmas 2014.

Act 5 - Aftermath

Although, as I write this, some six months and more after the extension was finished, we have not seen Big Mick and crew for a good while, we did see them off and on in the weeks following that Christmas.

Some of the issues we encountered were frustrating at the time, but insignificant in the great scheme of things. So, in the utility room Big Mick had built into the large downstairs space, the fuse that fed our washing machine and drier blew. But it did not just blow, it heated up and melted into the white plastic socket that surrounded it. In vain did I try to gouge out what remained.

"Poor materials", Big Mick advised me, before replacing the box, seemingly forgetting he had chosen them.

This bizarrely rapid onset of builder's amnesia continued. So, to my consternation, twice more in rapid succession we encountered water coming through our new ceiling. Fortunately, on each occasion, not much more than a trickle. On the first occasion, George the Cat broke all previous feats of endurance by slithering his way up the shallow false fireplace above the new hearth, from where he could just about reach a waste pipe that fed down from our shower above. It transpired the water was emanating from here.

"Poor fitting", he advised us, on what I was sure had been Big Mick's work.

On the second occasion, the leak came from the roof, and was down to a cracked tile, exacerbated by new guttering – closer to the trees and shrubbery than any we'd had before – that Marzena and I had allowed to become clogged with detritus.

"Cracked tile", Big Mick advised us, again seemingly unaware that, presumably, his team may have had something to do with it. On the other hand, Big Mick had done an absolutely sterling job removing old tiles from the out of sight rear roof and transporting them to the more visible front roof extension, so it blended in better. It would have been churlish in the extreme to have complained about a single cracked tile.

In another episode, floor tiles in one of the new en-suite bathrooms began to chip and crack. Konrad – our handyman friend who did not know how to name his price – rectified the problem whilst working on some other bits and bobs that needed to be done post-project. He spotted the cause: no plywood had been laid beneath the tiles, meaning they rested on an uneven surface. Big Mick did not demur when we fed this information back to him. One of his favourite pastimes was criticising his own workers – usually the temporary ones – to us. The young lad who had fitted the tiles in this en-suite bathroom had been a particular target of his. His crime was one of proceeding too slowly. At the time, Marzena and I had felt rather aggrieved on this young chap's behalf. He did work slowly, but steadily and precisely. It was he who was responsible for the blue and white effect in that bathroom. However, one thing we had observed during the course of the extension was that, with a few notable exceptions (mostly plumbing-related), Big Mick had a keen eye for what worked and did not when it came to building work. He had spotted something he did not like in this young man's approach, and appeared to have been right after all.

It was in vain we tried to explain, from time to time, that by one reckoning a mistake by one of his workers was a mistake on Big Mick's own part; after all, he had employed the labour. Big Mick would acknowledge this, but then proceed to critique the work of the individual in question with such passion that we began to sympathise with his plight. We began to think it really was difficult to get quality labourers. It seemed a clever ploy: so many Polish plumbers and tilers and brickies and plasterers and painters and others came and went, that it was relatively easy to speak ill of the departed. In reality, I think it was much more straightforward, and not a ploy at all: Big Mick was genuinely disappointed when, others having let him down, he had to let us down.

The frequency of incidents reduced, ending one day – literally! – with a bang when a drain cover Big Mick had fitted to replace the one buckled by the endless train of skip lorries, collapsed under my car wheel the second or third time I crossed it. I gingerly reversed the car out of the hole beneath, and subsequently told Big Mick in no uncertain terms I needed a new, steel drain cover – not the rusty second-hand one he'd had lying around and offered me.

A sturdy, silver-coloured cover was duly fitted, whereupon Big Mick, George the Cat, and the steady stream of casual labour they employed, faded from our lives. They will return at some point, no doubt, to fill a few cracks in the walls that have developed as the extension settles into position. And then, that will be it.

The truth is we will miss Big Mick and his entourage. Though at times palpitation-inducing, having them work on a project this size was an education, not only in building work, but in becoming more familiar with the mini-Polish world which now exists in this country. Marzena, in particular, will miss her daily chats in Polish about the state of the nations – British and Polish.

As for the building work, with the benefit of hindsight Big Mick did a fine job in sometimes difficult circumstances. Many of the problems encountered were not of his making, and he found a solution for every one – as well as giving generously of his time to steer us in the right direction on the extension. Further, Big Mick *did* return to put right post-project snags, as he had always promised he would - and continues to help us out on smaller jobs. We have recommended Big Mick since.

For my part, there remains just one hangover, not only from working with Big Mick, but also Szymon before him, the builder in Pinner. Namely, I have developed a Pavlovian sensitivity to the sound of running water – or anything remotely similar. Even the ticking clock in our living-room can trick me into thinking a torrent is on its way. In our garage, I have plastered on the wall, next to the main water feed, an idiot's guide to turning it off. For speed of access, a small stepladder stands permanently in front of the feed, which sits high on the wall. Post-extension (and post-diluvian), I am a man poised at any time to leap like a superhero into our garage, bolt up the stepladder... and turn off the main stopcock.

It may be I am now the one and only Englishman *not* willing to engage the services of the fabled, Polish plumber.

Part III - The All-Girl Polish Book Club

In *Polska Dotty* there is a chapter entitled *What the Poles Think About Us.* I endeavoured to make it a good introduction to the subject. But the "Us" in the chapter heading refers to many nations. In other words, what Poles think about Brits – but also Americans, Germans, Russians and so on. Now that so many Poles have come to the UK, I thought we should hear from them in more detail on the subject of Britain and the Brits.

Not that we know nothing. I already mentioned the Polish IT consultant whose blog became an overnight sensation. He mentioned some of the by now familiar observations and criticisms of the British way of life, such as why the heck do we have separate hot and cold taps? And milk with tea, and chips with vinegar? He also had a go at the UK's education system – as we have seen, it ranks way below Poland's – and the price of train tickets.

And now a little something for our Polish readers... Everything you always wanted to know about Britain but were too afraid to ask

The Guardian

That was in 2014. Eight years earlier – anticipating the bafflement of Polish immigrants – Laura Barton wrote in *The Guardian* on "Everything [Poles] always wanted to know about Britain but were too afraid to ask", with a handy translation into Polish. Many of the same topics came up - two taps instead of one, vinegar on chips, and expensive train fares. Also, why do Brits ask how you are if they don't care? Why are they all so obsessed with sunbathing? And – worryingly for me – where have all their plumbers gone?

But do Poles agree with Lucy Barton, and the IT consultant, on the nature of the British condition? Can we dig deeper into the subject? There was only one place to find out...

The All-Girl Polish Book Club began several years ago when a bunch of Polish girlfriends in our local town decided to get together every month or two to discuss Polish language books they had read. Marzena is a relative ingénue, having only joined in the last year or two. Though menfolk are not invited, and therefore I have no first-hand evidence of proceedings, I am led to believe debate is vigorous and intellectual. Certainly the attendees are! So could they throw some light on the British way of life?

We hosted a special Book Club evening for some of the members. One or two of the girls have English husbands, but all of our guests this night were Polish. Anetta "with 2 Ts", as we call her, a teaching assistant, attended with her husband Robert. Aneta "with one T", who works for an agency in the public sector, attended with her husband, Ryszard (Richard). Dominika – another teaching assistant, also came. And, of course, there was Marzena. As best we could, in what turned out to be a flowing conversation, we divided up the subject thematically.

Arrival in UK, preconceptions

There was a good chronological mix amongst our guests. Aneta and Ryszard had arrived in the UK in 2002, Anetta and Robert in 2004 – the year in which Poland joined the EU. Dominika and her husband came in 2007. As those of you familiar with *Polska Dotty* will know, Marzena and I returned to the UK in 1999, after two years living in Poland.

Poles are famous for their wanderlust, and this was apparent amongst our guests. Anetta and Robert had actually been living for three years in Canada when visa restrictions meant they had to consider their next move. They thought of going to the US, but a job opportunity for Robert took them to UK. The fact we speak English here helped them make their decision. Aneta did not speak good English on arrival, but came here anyway having spent the previous six months in the US. Ryszard had been living in Norway. Dominika's husband had also lived abroad – but in his case, it was eight months in England, so the place was familiar to him.

The English language was a big attraction for most of the girls. Dominika, for example, had been teaching English in Poland. I sensed from the conversation they felt this gave them a bit of a head start, an early confidence. The importance they attached to proficiency in the language became a theme of the evening's discussion, which was an eye-opener for me. We English are spoilt in this regard, of course.

I also sensed an economic imperative in their decision to come to the UK. It had been difficult at the time to find well-paid jobs in Poland.

Another reason was the simple need for a life change.

But plans were not well laid. None of the couples had had a concrete idea of how long they would stay in the UK. For Dominika and her husband, it might have been no more than four years, when her eldest of two boys was due to start school. For Anetta and Robert, the envisaged timescale, if any, was no more than a couple of years.

Language was again prominent when it came to preconceptions of UK life. Anetta and Aneta shared an impression of a posh language spoken by posh people. A world of Sherlock Holmes and Dickens (and no doubt these days, Downton Abbey, which is extremely popular in Poland). Generally, of smartly-dressed, upright people in suits and ties, saying please and thank you. I imagine we soon shattered those illusions!

But there were also more mundane preconceptions, and concerns. What about the fog? And driving on the left? Or – god forbid – both at the same time? And the terrible food..?

First impressions, later impressions

Most of our Polish friends' first impressions of UK life had endured, though, perhaps inevitably, they had grown used to certain aspects that had at first seemed difficult. Maybe this was resignation; maybe some things were an acquired taste.

Our guests were not averse to criticising our funny ways, as we shall see – but the consensus view was very positive…

So, Dominika thought life here was simply easier and more "sensible" than in Poland. Here, people looked for solutions; in Poland, they looked for… restrictions. Even down to small things, such as parking in the street. In Poland, in contrast to the UK, there were endless restrictions on street parking, Dominika explained.

Here, people seemed happier, and maybe as a consequence, were friendlier and smiled more. They said "hello". They helped – maybe with your pushchair. They didn't just ignore you.

Aneta continued in the same vein. Brits are very welcoming, she said. Arriving in the UK without much English, she began work in a rather rough pub in Holloway, where she found the staff and clientele friendly and supportive. A regular Irish customer bought her a book on English legends. A cockney chatted her up whilst another guest translated his rhyming slang (Aneta couldn't understand a word).

But Aneta was also shocked at just how rough the area was. For example, no-one checked tickets on the bus unless accompanied by the police. Marzena agreed with the sentiment, adding there was much division in the UK, both between classes and ethnic communities; some communities had become almost ghettoised.

Overall, though, Aneta and Ryszard really appreciated British culture, agreeing with Dominika. Aneta found the locals friendly and sociable. Ryszard and she had made many local friends. Richard found life here more straightforward. For example, he was amazed how trusting and lacking in bureaucracy the banks were when he first arrived and needed to set up an account. He also found the Brits more polite, and now Poles seemed almost rude in comparison. The UK was a better place to live he opined – both economically, and culturally. It was more tolerant.

But it could also be a puzzle! Before he left Canada, Robert asked his new employer what the dress code was in the UK. "Business casual", he was told, only to find, on arrival – commensurate with the preconception our friends had of posh Brits – everyone at work wore a tie. He'd had to make a frantic search for his. Equally perplexing, Robert and Anetta found they were not too far from their local school and playground, but there was no direct route to get to them. A shortcut would have solved the problem, but here in the UK, an Englishman's home is his castle, and woe betide anyone who walks too close to someone else's property. At this point, there was a general and wise nodding of heads, and for the first time during the evening, I felt like the odd one out. In Poland, it was agreed, by all Poles present, there was generally a better network of shortcuts...

Likes & dislikes

As lists seem to be the order of the day here – milk with tea, vinegar on chips, and so on – here is mine, based on the discussions we had. Views expressed were not necessarily universal to all our Polish friends... and I have added a word or two of explanation, where appropriate, in italics. As follows:

Likes

1. As already mentioned, people try to resolve issues straightforwardly; there is a general lack of bureaucracy compared to Poland.
2. Fairness in work, right from interview stage. Candidates are judged in the round, with less emphasis on academic achievement than in Poland. In contrast, for the equivalent of some UK positions that don't require high level qualifications, a PhD would be needed in Poland. Integrity at work is also important right from the start, whereas getting a job in Poland can sometimes be more a case of who you know rather than what you know.
3. A volunteer culture. In Poland, you charge for your work, or the "volunteering" is made obligatory.
4. Respect in British politics, even where politicians disagree. *In Poland, the standard of debate can sink very low, to the level of personal insults and derogatory language. At least one of our guests said it is now difficult to watch such exchanges when they come up on TV.*

5. The BBC, and TV news generally. *In Poland, nothing quite like the Beeb exists, and* all *channels feature advertising breaks.*
6. Free museums. *Entry to Polish museums is usually free for just one day per week.*
7. Public transport. *In Poland, trains and buses used to be rather decrepit, which may be what our guests – all of whom have been in the UK a long time – were recalling. Of late, public transport in Poland has improved significantly.*
8. Religious tolerance. *As we know, Catholicism dominates the religious scene in Poland, and has a sizeable influence on politics and the state in general. Along with its more conservative elements, including the controversial Radio Maryja, this does not necessarily make for a society tolerant of other religions.*

Why a Pole's politeness can be lost in translation

Mail Online

Dislikes

1. Over-education of the very young, starting them at school at the age of five. *In Poland, school traditionally began at seven, though this is being changed to six.*
2. Political correctness. *As the Mail Online reported in 2012, based on a study coming out of Portsmouth University, Poles speak in a more direct manner than Brits; "PC" can only exacerbate misunderstandings!*

3. Health & safety excess. *This is something we Brits complain about too. However, seeing as – according to official statistics – the UK has one of the best health & safety records in Europe, and Poland one of the worst, maybe we shouldn't complain too much.*
4. The exorbitant price of tickets for the arts, which makes regular visits to the theatre/opera/ballet unaffordable. *In contrast, in Poland, the arts (including the performing arts) are well-funded, particularly at a local level, making for more affordable prices on the door.*
5. Inferior building standards. *A criticism which I can only put down to a need for more robust standards in Poland, where the weather is, of course, more extreme.*
6. And, of course, separate hot and cold taps. And carpet in the bathroom. *Not much need for explanation here, other than to say it has been one of Marzena's priorities to rip out the separate hot and cold taps and carpet, in every bathroom of every home in which we have ever lived in the UK – and replace them with mixer taps and tiled floors. With a plethora of Polish builders now living in the UK, I suspect separate hot and cold taps and bathroom carpets will soon become a thing of the past, perhaps appearing on Antiques Roadshow from time to time and attracting high valuations.*

Important note for the reader: I reserved my position when it came to respect in British politics, and had to be picked up off the floor when our system of public transport was praised.

The British character

Having been picked up off the floor, we went on to address the British character. What did our Polish friends make of Brits, and British attitudes toward Polish immigrants?

Again, opinions were largely positive. Ryszard remarked on his 70-year-old neighbour, who remembered the contribution made by Poles during the Second World War – but who on the other hand complained that, more recently, Poles had taken British jobs. Aneta felt Brits were particularly tolerant, again of her initially poor English, but also generally. Marzena agreed. She could not imagine Poland taking a million Brits with the relative equanimity that Britain had taken that number of Poles. There was general agreement on this. Anetta was of the opinion that the attitude of Brits to immigrant Poles has eased up. Maybe at first there were suspicions, but now practically everyone had come into contact with Poles, there seemed to be general acceptance of their status.

Dominika made an interesting observation on the British work ethic. As we have seen, our Polish friends were impressed at the British sense of fair play that permeated work, making for pleasant working conditions. But she was less impressed at the lack of diligence of British workers. She noted that some workers were assertive, which manifested itself in a sort of "go slow" mentality. In other words, do what you have to do, and don't race through. If you do, you'll only find on the other side either more work, or none – in which case, you'll seem not busy enough. Marzena agreed. Back home, many Poles even had two jobs, because needs must. Our own experience with the hard-working Big Mick and his men only corroborated this, not forgetting Konrad and Bartek, who could complete multiple sizeable jobs in one (long) day.

Polish "ghettoes"

I decided to touch on something a little more sensitive, and ask if Poles who had come here in the recent wave had settled into ghettoes. That had been a conclusion of some academic studies, and a criticism in some sections of the press - particularly as Poles had come here with an advantage over some other immigrants, in that they shared a similar credo with the native Brits. This brought out quite a reaction – the same reaction – from all present. But it was not aimed at the British. Rather, as Dominika remarked, there is a cadre of recent immigrant Poles in this country who are disrespectful toward the British. They term Brits the pejorative "Angol" – difficult to translate but probably something akin to "Limey" (or worse). These types of Poles, pretty much lacking in mentality, *do* remain in a ghetto, and have no intention of mixing with the locals. Aneta agreed with Dominika, and castigated such Poles in no uncertain terms. For herself, she was always trying to make friends with the locals.

On the other hand – and there was a to and fro to much of the evening's discussion – Anetta considered there was another type of Pole who *did* wish to mix with Brits. In any case, it was natural enough that many Poles here gravitated toward other Poles. Marzena agreed. She said Poles are pretty good at mixing, and for many of those who didn't it may be because of their inadequate English. Other ethnic communities in the UK, who have been established here much longer, still did not mix with Brits as much as Poles do.

The old country

What did the group miss most – and least or not at all – about Poland? At this point, I anticipated a list akin to their likes and dislikes of the British way of life. And sure enough, the conversation started off in such fashion. The girls, in particular, most missed their friends, including in some cases best friends left behind in Poland. All our guests missed Poland – Polish places. But then, the conversation took a profound and philosophical turn, raising the question - what *is* home?

After some discussion, Dominika reached an interesting conclusion - that home is a state of mind, rather than a place. So, when she flies back to Poland for holidays, she steps off the plane and takes a first, deep breath. Soon, she is at her parents' house, sitting on the back balcony with them enjoying a cup of coffee, looking out at the view. "This experience is home", she said. Anetta held a similar view, not yet quite feeling that the UK was "home", or at least, if it was, Poland was equally so. Marzena – to my relief – regarded the UK as home – but then, she had been here the longest and was married to a Brit. Poland was still an emotional tie, she said, but no longer home.

Others saw it more practically. Home is here, Robert said, where we have our walls, our life. Here, in the UK, is our normal, day-to-day life, where we know how to get around – and that equates to home. Aneta and Ryszard agreed that home is here in the UK. Ryszard, from spending time working on the outside of his house, had got to know all the neighbours, whom he now regarded as friends. Poland, Aneta said – amongst other things – represented problems, including sometimes poor family relations (presumably exacerbated by distance).

Though Dominika's true home was still Poland, she did not miss one aspect: the twitching curtains. This is something I described in *Polska Dotty* – the almost unhealthy interest neighbours take in each other. Dominika appreciated the freedom of the UK way of life.

Anetta had a different perspective. Growing up in a city in Poland, she was not used to being watched. In fact, she is more used to this over here, where they are the only Polish family on their estate.

Where did all this leave us concerning the concept of "home" and its location (geographical or otherwise)? To answer this, tongue in cheek, I introduced our guests to Norman Tebbit's infamous "cricket test", adapted somewhat. So, if Poland were to play England at football, who would they support? For most of them it was clear – Poland, of course!

Knowing what's good for me, I left the last word to Marzena. She was of the opinion that home is, ultimately, where your children settle, and this was likely to be the UK for most of the recent wave of immigrant Poles. That led us seamlessly into the final part of our discussion...

The future

Attitudes to the old country had uncovered differences in opinions between couples, and even within couples. What the future held for our Polish friends – and the million or so like them who had arrived in the UK in the last ten years – would do so even more candidly.

Dominika kicked us off with a tale of friends of theirs who had returned to Poland after time in the UK, where they could not make a go of their business. They remained in Poland for a couple of years, but then came back to the UK, swearing they would never return to live in Poland again. And swearing *at* the Polish mentality and bureaucracy – the reason for their decision. On the other hand, Dominika's own sister lived for a period in Ireland, but had now gone back to Poland, where she would stay. She missed Polish life too much. Anetta told a similar story of a Polish girlfriend who went back to live in Poland with her children; she had not settled in the UK, where she had found the language difficult.

Marzena thought there was an element of luck involved in settling, and it depended who you encountered. The mothers at the school gates could be a pretty cliquey bunch. She had the good fortune to mix with other Central and Eastern Europeans – amongst them, a Slovakian, and a Georgian – Elene – who recommended Big Mick.

Endorsing what Marzena had said earlier, Anetta said she will likely follow her children, though I detected a desire to return to Poland if the time was right. Her husband Robert's view was subtly different – he said they might retire to Poland.

Aneta seemed genuinely ambivalent. Ryszard and she were probably the most effusive of all our guests about UK life, and yet Aneta considered what she would do if she could get a good job now in Poznan (her home town), with all her friends around. That would be a dilemma, because she now had such a network in the UK, too. Before I could chip in that, on balance, I suspected she might end up staying in the UK, Ryszard declared he would stay here. Here, he said, was a country run by normal rules, governed by normal relationships. Besides, their daughter was likely to remain in the UK. There you go, I thought. A moment later, Ryszard said he wasn't entirely sure where they'd retire to...

The future for immigrant Poles in the UK was proving elusive – as predicting the future usually is. Dominika elucidated the problem, by way of an example. Her boys had been at a summer camp in Poland. There, the other kids (presumably most if not all Polish) called them "Little Englishmen". At school in the UK, of course – camouflaged by their English accents but not their surnames – they were called "Poles"! As Dominika put it, they had no clear identity.

Marzena mentioned something similar. Her brother's family had settled in the UK a decade or so ago, and the eldest daughter had just begun at university. Still with a Polish passport, she was invited to the "foreigners' club". Schooled in the UK, and with her lilting North Yorkshire accent, she felt mildly insulted.

Robert had the last word. Yes, it all made sense – that the future meant the children, and they'd all likely follow theirs around. That could mean the UK, could mean Poland – who knew? On the other hand, the south of France would be nice...

Afterword

What will become of the million or so Poles who have entered the UK in the last ten years remains an open question, of course, and one that fascinates me. I don't suppose many will drift to the south of France, or anywhere else. Instead, I think most will remain here, and continue, little by little, to influence our way of life, even as they adapt to it.

Whilst this remains an imponderable, maybe it is better to take stock of the Polish influx. For me, it is best described as a kaleidoscopic experience: complex, constantly shifting, but with discernible patterns – and extremely colourful.

I hope some of that colour has been transmitted to you through this book. Also that those without much experience of interaction with Poles – though there can't be many of you left! – will understand better, and be more understanding of, the Polish immigrants you meet.

In the meantime, enjoy our Polish minority, now one of the most significant ethnic groups in the UK.

Enjoy their delis, packed full of traditional Polish food including *paczki* doughnuts, much lighter and tastier than our own.

Enjoy their waiters, bartenders, and hotel staff, who will serve you with quiet efficiency and a willingness to please.

Enjoy their doctors, who will actually give you the time of day – not simply prescribe paracetamol.

Enjoy the mathematical prowess of the average Polish teacher and teaching assistant; it's bound to be better than your own, and a benefit to your kids.

Enjoy their builders and handymen, every one a factotum, the living personification of *Polak potrafi* – a Pole can do.

Enjoy their cleaners, who will wipe and reorganise your possessions with such vigour you won't recognise the home when you return.

And enjoy their hairdressers, who will guarantee you a coiffure of red hennaed hair – a precondition for entry onto the premises.

Just do me one, small favour, please...

Enjoy their plumbing more than I did.

Acknowledgements

My thanks to:

Anthony Casey for his precise editing, and inspiration, working on the text (check out his website: http://inside-poland.com);

Liam O'Farrell for his wonderful illustrations (his website can be found at www.liamofarrell.com);

Grzegorz Nowak for his continuing assistance with the *Polska Dotty* website;

The many Poles who took the bold step to come to the UK, and in doing so made this book possible; and

Marzena, Natalia and Liliana, my sine qua non.

Jonathan Lipman
May 2016

About the Author

Jonathan Lipman was born in Oxfordshire, England in 1968. In the 1980s he encountered many temporary émigrés from Eastern Europe - including Russians, Romanians and... Poles. They were visitors to his father's team that pioneered wind energy in the UK. Conversations with them would range far and wide, from the flaws in Capitalism to the evils of Communism, from the corrupt West to the post-Communist "Wild East", from Keynes to Marx and Engels. Little did Jonathan know this would stand him in good stead when, at the age of 25, he'd meet a variety of Eastern Europeans on a course at Oxford University, and fall in love with one of them - a Pole.

After qualifying as a lawyer in 1997, Jonathan married Marzena in Krakow, Poland, and they spent the next two years getting to grips with Warsaw. Jonathan worked for a renowned and very Polish law firm; Marzena completed her doctorate. All this is the subject of Jonathan's first book – *Polska Dotty*. In 1999 they returned to the UK, and after Poland joined the EU in 2004, found themselves surrounded by a flood of new Polish immigrants – the inspiration for *Polska Dotty 2*.

Jonathan and Marzena live in Buckinghamshire, England, where they are preparing for a more traditional flood by way of two girls, two cats, two fish, and (apparently) at least two of every generation of apple device ever built.

Polska Dotty

About the Book

Are you travelling to Poland, and wish to know more about the Poles you'll encounter? Are you fascinated by this country of forty million, rich in natural beauty, cultured, and famous for its people's wanderlust? Have you ever wondered what makes your Polish plumber or waitress or doctor over here tick? What book do you pick for background and insight? A superficial travel guide? A dry history book?

No! You need the genre-busting Polska Dotty. Follow the hilarious exploits of a newly-wed English lad and Polish girl as they settle in Poland and encounter corrupt Polish police, counterfeit software sellers, and scammy private doctors. Observe as Jonathan, under the watchful eye of Marzena, gets to grips with the Polish condition, and finally integrates - completing his rite of passage by learning how to down tumblers of vodka in one mighty gulp.

Polska Dotty informs about every aspect of Polish society including its work ethic, family values, and the Polish character itself. This is a funny, heartfelt, sparkling read, a touching portrayal of an Englishman's submersion into Polish life.

Reviews

"An utterly charming story of the ups and downs of an Englishman who tries to assimilate into a completely different world" - Cooltura

"A cracking read... really is one of a kind" - Krakow Polska

"A colorful introduction to Poland for readers who know little of the country" - Warsaw Voice

"Guaranteed to offer invaluable advice and lots of laughs" - Inside Poland

"Full of the kind of anecdotes that anyone who has moved to Poland from the UK will recognise instantly" - Krakow Post

"A sympathetic insight into Polish society... a charming and informative book" - Hubert Zawadzki, co-author, A Concise History of Poland

"Wonderful personal observations" - Cosmopolitan Review

AVAILABLE IN E-BOOK AND PAPERBACK ON AMAZON

Printed in Great Britain
by Amazon